BEYOND PREWRATH

END-TIME PROPHECY

Robert Parker

Robert's Trumpet
www.RobertsTrumpet.com

To my loving parents

BEYOND PREWRATH OVERVIEW

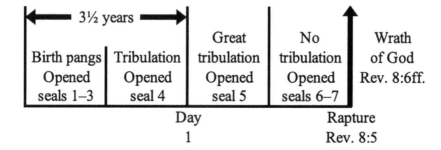

Table of Contents

Acknowledgements.. vii

Preface ix

Abbreviations... x

Definitions xii

Introduction: List of Book's Theses, Proofs, and Positions 1

Chapter 1: Premillennial and Seventy Weeks of Daniel 9

Chapter 2: New Understandings.. 21

Chapter 3: Seventh Opened Seal and Silence in Heaven 31

Chapter 4: Daniel 8:13–14: 2,300 Evenings and Mornings...................... 49

Chapter 5: Daniel Parallels and Goat-Ram Timeline................................ 61

Chapter 6: Parallels between Matthew 24 and Revelation 6–8 69

Chapter 7: The Eschatological Day of the Lord: About Day 1 89

Chapter 8: Beyond Day 1: Eschatological Day of the Lord and Day of Christ........ 107

Chapter 9: The Eighth Head and the Multiple Kingdom Coalition 125

Chapter 10: Signs of the End of the Age 137

Chapter 11: Millennium, Resurrection, and Beyond................................141

Chapter 12: Final Thoughts 153

Subject Index 159

Scripture Index 161

About the Author 169

List of Figures

Beyond Prewrath Overview iv
Figure 1: Second Coming of Jesus Events.. 10
Figure 2: Five Rapture Positions 13
Figure 3: Darkness, Blood, and Fire.. 21
Figure 4: Seventh Opened Seal Conceptual Timeline 34
Figure 5: Silence in Heaven Calculated... 36
Figure 6: Rapture and Wrath 40
Figure 7: Seventh Opened Seal Timeline 41
Figure 8: Three Great Eschatological Theophanies 44
Figure 9: Timelines for Sixth and Seventh Opened Seals................................... 59
Figure 10: Parallels between Daniel 2, 7, 8, 10, Matthew 24, and Revelation 6 63
Figure 11: Timeline of the Beast of the Sea... 66
Figure 12: Parallels between Matthew 24 and Revelation 6–8 70
Figure 13: Timeline of Start of the Seventieth Week of Daniel 71
Figure 14: Seven Earthquakes 74
Figure 15: Fourth and Fifth Opened Seals (Tribulation and Great Tribulation)........ 76
Figure 16: Sixth and Seventh Opened Seals (No Tribulation) 82
Figure 17: Beyond Prewrath Overview Timeline.. 86
Figure 18: Chronology of Eschatological Events around Day 1 92
Figure 19: Jesus's Visit and Jerusalem Campaign... 95
Figure 20: Satan on Day 1 98
Figure 21: Babylon Attacked 100
Figure 22: Man of Lawlessness Revealed 105
Figure 23: The First Eschatological Day of Christ and Third Day of the Lord 109
Figure 24: The Fourth Eschatological Day of the Lord and Fifth Blown Trumpet .. 110
Figure 25: Jehoshaphat Campaign.. 113
Figure 26: Updated Three Great Eschatological Theophanies 116
Figure 27: Eschatological Days of the Lord and of Christ Overview 122
Figure 28: Jesus's Eschatological Warfare Campaigns....................................... 123
Figure 29: Eight Heads (Empires) 135
Figure 30: Earth's Twisted Crust and the New Earth.. 143
Figure 31: Populating Earth and Heaven.. 145

Acknowledgements

A special thanks to my eschatology teacher, who directed me as I studied end-time events and calculations. After seeing chapter 3, he recommended I write a book. A special thanks to my friend Karen, who reviewed the developing manuscript almost every weekend for about six months. A special thanks to my church classmates, who listened to my presentations, as well as others who reviewed the manuscript.

Thank you to my 2021–2022 eschatology teacher Mike a graduate of Dallas Theological Seminary who was supportive in my book. Also, my brother Dave who helped sharpen my skills in prophecy phone call debates, though whom I have not yet changed from his pretribulation view.

Preface

This book provides dramatic new eschatological understandings of the end-time prophecies found throughout the Bible and connects them together to show a timeline of events. But why should anyone bother to study something as esoteric as end-time prophecy? Well, the first reason is the promise that you will be blessed for it (Rev. 1:3). Who does not want to be blessed? The second reason is that every verse of Scripture is the inspired word of God, which should be studied and taught (2 Tim. 3:16a). Third, why would God give us the bleak message of a great tribulation? The only reasonable answer is that our loving God wants us to be forewarned and prepared against false prophets—the deception that will be rampant during the seventieth week of Daniel. Being forewarned, we will not to be led astray from the truth and will be waiting for the sign of His coming. Unfortunately, some who are not knowledgeable of Scripture may fall away into the deception of apostasy. This book describes the signs of Christ's return and will hopefully help explain the seemingly esoteric eschatology of the Bible, preparing us for the man of lawlessness and Antichrist.

Corrections from the first book in 2021 include: (1) The Antichrist is the first beast of Revelation 13, (2) Israel is likely to be raptured in Revelation 11:19 to Jerusalem for the béma judgment then later to heaven versus immediately to heaven, (3) figures iv and 17 for the sixth and seventh opened seals changed from "no wrath" to "no tribulation," and (4) it is unclear whether the man of lawlessness will enter through the temple's eastern outer wall known as the Golden Gate or some other gate.

Abbreviations

The abbreviation Day 1 is used by far the most frequently for the start date of these events. It refers to when the abomination of destruction of the temple occurs, which ends the twice-daily temple sacrifices. This then begins the great tribulation for the Gentiles and Jacob's trouble for the Jewish tribes. The 1,290 and 1,335 days of Daniel 12:11–12 count from Day 1.

1 Cor.	1 Corinthians
1 Thess.	1 Thessalonians
1 Tim.	1 Timothy
2 Cor.	2 Corinthians
2 Sam.	2 Samuel
2 Thess.	2 Thessalonians
2 Tim.	2 Timothy
B5	fifth poured bowl
cf.	compare
ch.	chapter
Dan.	Daniel
Day 1	middle of the seventieth week of Daniel
Day 1,260	end of the seventieth week of Daniel
Eph.	Ephesians
Ex.	Exodus
Ezek.	Ezekiel
ff.	and following
Gal.	Galatians
Gen.	Genesis
Hab.	Habakkuk
Heb.	Hebrews
Hos.	Hosea
Isa.	Isaiah
Jer.	Jeremiah

Lev.	Leviticus
Mal.	Malachi
Matt.	Matthew
Mt.	Mount
Neh.	Nehemiah
Num.	Numbers
Phil.	Philippians
Pss.	Psalms
Rev.	Revelation
Rom.	Romans
S5	fifth opened seal
S6	sixth opened seal
T5	fifth blown trumpet
T6	sixth blown trumpet
v.	verse
vv.	verses
Zech.	Zechariah
Zeph.	Zephaniah

Definitions

Chiastic structure: It is a poetic writing style in which a sequence of thoughts is presented and then repeated in reverse order. For example, ABBA (Mark 2:27), ABCCBA (Matt. 6:24). Though there does not need to be a repeated middle theme, e.g., ABA (1 Cor. 11:27–29) or ABCBA (Matt. 11:28–30).

> And he said to them, "The Sabbath was made for man, not man for the Sabbath. (Mark 2:27)

Eschatology: A branch of theology about final things, such as the second coming of Jesus; separation of the wicked (to eternal death) and the righteous (to eternal life); the millennium, and eternity.

Septet: A septet is a group of seven similar things. In reference to eschatology: seven opened seals, seven blown trumpets, and seven poured bowls. Unless noted otherwise, references to septet will be in relation to these three sets of septets. There are other eschatological one-time septets, such as the seven lampstands – churches (Rev. 2–3), seven thunders (Rev. 10:3), seven earthquakes (figure 14), and seven eschatological days of the Lord (figure 27). These others appear to occur during the three sets of septets.

Introduction

List of Book's Theses, Proofs, and Positions

The following provides a list of theses, proofs, and position descriptions of the most important parts of the book.

I. NEW PREMILLENNIAL POSITION THESES

Beyond Prewrath is a new premillennial position based on the following four major theses:

1) The church will enter that second half of the seventieth week of Daniel to experience Antichrist's great tribulation.

2) The rapture of the church (for the righteous) and the wrath of God (against the wicked) will occur on the same day as in the days of Noah and Lot (Luke 17:22–30).

3) The three–time, scripturally unique theophany phrase in Scripture of "peals of thunder, rumblings, flashes of lightning, and an earthquake" has a rapture meaning. Lightning will be proposed to represent the metaphorical arm of Jesus rapturing those to the sky. An analogy can be made to Elijah's chariots of fire.

4) Each of the three septets are considered chronological with no overlap.

A septet is a group of seven similar things. Each theophany occurs at the end of each respective Revelation septet. That is, each theophany occurs in the seventh opened seal (Rev. 8:5), seventh blown trumpet (Rev. 11:19), and seventh poured bowl (Rev. 16:18). The first septet will be proposed to be the rapture of the elect to heaven, the second septet the rapture of Israel to Jerusalem, and third septet the rapture of the sheep (righteous). It is unclear when the goats (wicked) are judged and therefore whether they are part of the third septet rapture.

If these four theses are demonstrated, then the rapture of the church cannot be pretribulation or prewrath, which are both before the end of first septet in Revelation 8:5. This thesis agrees with the posttribulation rapture position that the end of the seventieth week of Daniel, Israel would be raptured though not to heaven but to Jerusalem for the béma judgment. See chapters 2, 3 and 8.

II. TWO NEW PROOFS AGAINST THE PRETRIBULATION

Two new proofs against the pretribulation will be shown based on the following:

1) There is no exact rapture theophany phrase "peals of thunder, rumblings, flashes of lightning, and an earthquake" (Rev. 2 or 3) before John arrives in heaven, as in the first three septets of Revelation 8:5, 11:19, and 16:18.

2) There is no multitude rejoicing in heaven (Rev. 4 or 5) when John goes to heaven, as associated with Scripture in the first (Revelation 7:9–17) and third (Revelation 19:1–4) septets.

Consider there are already three existing proofs from the prewrath community in 2 Thessalonians 2:2–5, based on two respective events which must occur before the day of the Lord (see chapter 2). The fifth being Matthew 24:29 that the elect must endure the great tribulation. So, there are now five strong proofs.

III. JOEL 2:28–32 IS IN THE SIXTH BLOWN TRUMPET

Joel 2:28–32 and its parallel Acts 2:17–21 are located in the sixth blown trumpet and not the sixth opened seal based on the following major theses: Darkness, blood, and fire are only mentioned in the Jehoshaphat campaign, which is part of the sixth blown trumpet. To support this, several parallels are shown between Revelation 9:13–19, 14:14–20, and other scriptures. The sixth opened seal of Revelation 6:12–17 has no blood and fire (see chapter 2). This new interpretation opens the door for the rapture occurring later than prewrath. Beyond prewrath chapter 3 has Revelation 7:9–17, with the multitude in heaven rejoicing being considered the consequence of the sequentially previous earthly rapture in Revelation 8:5.

IV. 2 THESSALONIANS 2:2–5 ESCHATOLOGICAL DAY OF THE LORD

This day of the Lord is in reference to the middle of the seventieth week of Daniel (Day 1) based on the following:

1) Scholars' understanding of 2 Thessalonians 2:2–5 is that the apostle Paul may have missed the rapture since they associate it with that same day of the Lord. Any scriptural interpretation of Paul missing the rapture should be without merit.

2) So, how can Paul enter into this day of the Lord without missing the rapture? The only apparent solution is for there to be an earlier and separate eschatological day of the Lord. This earlier day will be proposed to be Day 1, represented by the Jerusalem campaign of Jesus in Zechariah 14:1–10. Their apparent concern in asking Paul the question is the likely same–day temple abomination of desolation and attack by Gog with massive death and exile. On that same day Jesus appears to be roused into what is considered a counterattack against Gog (see chapter 7).

3) Events of Daniel 9:27 and 2 Thessalonians 2:2–5 are interpreted as as a reference to the same middle of the seventieth week. Daniel has the abomination of desolation in the middle of the seventieth week. 2 Thessalonians 2:3–4 has the revealing of the man of lawlessness with him taking a seat in the temple in reference to the day of the Lord. An abomination of the temple would have worldwide attention, likely causing a revealing of the man of lawlessness.

V. SIXTH OPENED SEAL IS ABOUT 27 TO 32 DAYS LONG

A huge finding is the proposed duration of the sixth opened seal based on the following premises (see chapter 4):

1) Daniel 8:13–14 is where one holy one asks a question and the other holy one answers it. Since Scripture is exact, this then forms an equation of equality where the question equals the answer and can then be solved.

2) The left side of the equation (how long is the vision) is 1,335 days from Daniel 12:12.

3) The right side of the equation must include both days of light and when there is no light available for temple sacrifices it must include days of darkness. Days of light is 1,150 days from Daniel 8:14. The Expanded Bible supports both 1,150 and 2,300 days. Since the left side of the equation (1,335 days) must equal the right side of the equation (days of priestly light and darkness, which are both positive), this prevents Daniel 8:14 being interpreted as 2,300 days of priestly light.

$$1,335 \text{ days} \neq 2,300 \text{ days} + \text{days of darkness}$$

4) There are two unknown darkness durations in the equation: the sixth opened seal and the fifth poured bowl. The fifth poured bowl duration is tightly bound within the third septet of thirty days and includes the six other poured bowls. This tightly bound fifth poured bowl allows us to correspondingly tighten the sixth opened seal duration range.

5) Since Revelation 9:5 is 150 days of darkness, this by itself supports the sixth open seal duration being 35 days [1,335 - (1,150 + 150 + other days of darkness)] or less.

VI. DAY OF RAPTURE IS ON SEVENTH OR EIGHTH DAY

Another huge finding is that the rapture of the church will occur on either the seventh or eighth day in the seventh opened seal (see chapter 3). Some will reference Matthew 24:36 that no one knows the day or hour but only the Father. If we are honest with each other, we will recognize that this does not exclude the legitimate interpretation of being able to narrow it down to two days. Supporting reasons include:

1) According to Luke 17:22–30, prior to the rapture there is a time of planting and building. These events indicate daylight and peaceful activities that are different from the sixth opened seal of twenty–four–hour darkness and the wrath of the Lamb against the wicked.

2) Luke 17:22–30 also tells us that prior to the rapture, it will be a time of marriages. Previously, marriages were forbidden (1 Tim. 4:1–3). This indicates the Antichrist has temporarily lost control over those with the mark of the beast. Therefore, one would not expect any persecution.

3) Half an hour of silence in heaven (in Rev. 8:1) will be equated to seven and a half days on earth using Daniel's derived time ratio of 360 to 1 (seven Daniel years to one prophetic week). Genesis 7:4 and 10 of seven days prior to the flood (wrath of God), seems to provide merit that Luke 17:22–30 has a second meaning—beyond the rapture and day of the Lord occurring on the same day.

4) The multitude in heaven rejoicing (in Rev. 7:9–17) is a consequence of the earthly rapture (in Rev. 8:5). This interpretation of Revelation 8:5 chronologically before 7:9–17 is allowed since not all Scripture is chronological.

VII. ANTICHRIST APPEARS ON DAY 1

The Antichrist does not come into existence until Day 1 which is based on the following (see chapter 5):

1) Antichrist is a man represented by the man of lawlessness being indwelt by Satan. This is also a representation of Judas Iscariot who was indwelt by Satan. These two men seem to reflect the prophecy in Revelation 17:11: "As for the beast that was and is not, it is an eighth but it belongs to the seven, and it goes to destruction." Each man (beast) is called the son of destruction in John 17:12 (near prophecy of Jesus betrayal) and 2 Thessalonians 2:2–3 (far eschatological prophecy).

2) Satan is not thrown to earth until the heavenly battle of Revelation 12:7–17, and then a remnant of Israel is protected for 1,260 days. This protection ends at the end of the second septet with their theophany rapture in Revelation 11:19.

VIII. DIFFERENT NAMES OF THE MAN OF LAWLESSNESS

During the seventieth week of Daniel there are different names of the man of lawlessness depending on when and what he has authority over or whether Satan indwells within him. At the start of the seventieth week, he is called the little horn. During the first opened seal he is likely to give up his horn to become the man of lawlessness without a kingdom. This man of lawlessness is also called the son of destruction. On Day 1, Satan indwells within him and they become the Antichrist. Together with the ten horns, and seven heads with ten diadems it is called the beast of the sea. At the end of the Armageddon battle the man of lawlessness, called the beast, is thrown into the lake of fire. Satan is bound and thrown into a pit for a thousand years.

When the man of lawlessness is thrown into the lake of fire, Satan no longer is indwelt within him and therefore the Antichrist no longer exists. The Antichrist will have existed for three and a half years of Daniel (Day 1 to 1,260) plus the time up to the end of the sixth poured bowl (less than thirty days). This is a total of approximately 1,289 days of the Antichrist existence. See chapters 5, 9 and 11.

IX. THERE ARE SEVERAL UNIQUE DAYS OF THE LORD AND NOT JUST ONE

Almost all scholars consider there to be only one generic eschatological day of the Lord. It will be proposed that there are several unique days of the Lord based on the following major theses. If just one of the below is shown to be supported, then the theses of more than one day of the Lord will have been proven.

1) There are three warfare campaigns of Jesus (days of the Lord) that are separate and unique days of the Lord. Two are during darkness (Jerusalem and Jehoshaphat) and one is during light (Armageddon).

2) The duration of each day of the Lord is not the same since each we know some have different durations. For example, the fifth blown trumpet day of the Lord is 150 days long (Rev. 9:5), though Armageddon lasts for fewer than thirty days since it is interpreted within the third septet of poured bowls, lasting a total of thirty days.

3) Paul must be raptured before the same–day rapture and day of the Lord yet enter the day of the Lord, as described in 2 Thessalonians 2:1–5. By interpretation, this requires two separate days of the Lord.

4) Chapters 7 and 8 support the idea that there are at least seven chronologically different days of the Lord. They occur on: (1) Day 1 for the Jerusalem campaign (Ezek. 38; Zech. 14:1–11), (2) the sixth opened seal of the wrath of the Lamb (Rev. 6:16), (3) the elect rapture (Matt. 24:29–31 and Rev. 8:5), (4) the fifth blown trumpet (Rev. 9:5), (5) the sixth blown trumpet for the Jehoshaphat campaign (Rev. 9:13–19; 14:18–19; Joel 3:14), (6) the sixth poured bowl of

the Armageddon campaign (Rev. 16:12–16; 19:11–21), and (7) the seventh poured bowl (Rev. 16:18).

X. THE BEAST OF THE SEA

The Antichrist is considered the beast from the sea in Revelation 13:1–10, which is a correction from the 2021 publication. The beast has seven heads, ten horns, and ten diadems in Revelation 13:1. In Revelation 12:3 identified as a great red dragon. Daniel 7:24 has another (little horn) to rise out of the ten horns. So, we have the great red dragon and the beast associated with the ten horns, who will both be associated as the Antichrist.

The beast of the sea and the beast of the earth of Revelation 13 are equated to the three demonic spirits of Revelation 16:13–14 preparing for battle and in Revelation 19:20 these three demonic spirits are defeated. The three demonic spirits of Revelation 16:13 are the dragon (Satan), the beast, and the false prophet. Though how can two in Revelation 13 equate to three in Revelation 16 and 19–20?

The answer appears that the Antichrist represents two individuals and not just one. The man is proposed as the man of lawlessness, and the second as Satan who indwells and empowers him on Day 1. Together the two represent the Antichrist. The third individual of the demonic spirits is the false prophet. Therefore, Revelation 13 two beasts (beast of the sea and beast of the earth) can now be equated to the three demonic spirits of Revelation 16:13. See chapters 2, 5 and 9.

XI. SECOND AND THIRD THEOPHANIES

This book revision has a different understanding of the second and third theophanies. The Jewish remnant protection ends after 1,260 days in Revelation 12:6, 14, which is the end of the second septet. Since Israel is raptured in Revelation 11:19 (end of the second septet) it does not seem reasonable for them to be rejoicing in heaven eight chapters later in Revelation 19:1–5. Further analysis points to them being raptured in the second theophany horizontally to the béma location in Jerusalem and not to heaven initially. The elect would also be at the béma judgment. After the béma judgment would be the marriage supper followed by them participating in the Armageddon battle. After these events, it points to the righteous sheep of Matthew 25:31–36 taken in third theophany (Rev. 16:18) to be separately from the wicked goats. The sheep would also attend the supper.

XII. PARALLELS WITH REVELATION 16 AND 19

The sixth poured bowl of the Armageddon battle of Revelation 16:12–16 is proposed as the same battle as in Revelation 19:11–16, although through different eyes. Chapter 16 (identified as the sixth poured bowl in v. 17) has the three unclean spirits (dragon, beast, and false prophet) and separately the kings from the east traveling to enter the war. Chapter 19 has God entering the war, which would be expected to be immediate. The beast and false prophet are captured in Revelation 19:20. Satan, the dragon, was also captured in Revelation 20:1–3.

The same three unclean spirits in chapters 16 and 19 support this as the same chronological battle. These two chapters describing the same event then helps to provide support that the third rapture theophany of Revelation 16:18 in the seventh poured bowl could be chronologically occurring during Revelation 19.

Chapter 1

Premillennial and Seventy Weeks of Daniel

PREMILLENNIALISM AND AMILLENNIALISM

Premillennialism interprets Revelation 20:1–6 to mean that Jesus will physically return to earth to reign for a literal thousand years.[1] Amillennialism interprets this millennium as symbolic. Many amillennial denominations, such as Catholic, Eastern Orthodox, and Anglican, generally view this passage of Revelation as pertaining to the present time, when Christ reigns in heaven with the departed saints. This interpretation views Revelation as referring to a spiritual reign rather than a physical reign on earth. The amillennialist view is that the kingdom of Christ has been present in the church since the events of Pentecost in the book of Acts.

PAROUSIA—A COMING OR PRESENCE

Strong's Concordance defines the Greek noun *parousia* as "a presence," or "a coming"—though not necessarily the return of Christ.[2] Scripture verses associated with the coming of Christ include Matthew 24:3, 27; 1 Corinthians 15:23; 1 Thessalonians 2:19; 4:15; 5:23; James 5:8; and 1 John 2:28. But context is important. In 1 Corinthians 16:17, *parousia* is associated with the disciples. In 2 Thessalonians 2:9, we have the coming (*parousia*) of the lawless one.

The first *parousia* of Jesus was when He came as the Lamb of God, which encompasses different aspects of His life from birth until His ascension in Acts 1:6–11. The second *parousia* is when Jesus returns as a lion in Jeremiah 49:19, which will also involve different aspects of His presence and coming. In chapters 3, 7, and 8 of this book, the author will identify ten *parousia*

---

1   Wikipedia, s.v. "Premillennialism," accessed March 28, 2021, https://en.wikipedia.org/wiki/Premillennialism.
2   James Strong, *Strong's Exhaustive Concordance of the Bible*, Bible Hub, s.v. "3952 *parousia*," accessed March 31, 2021, https://biblehub.com/greek/3952.htm.

events during the Lord's second coming. See figure 1 for a list of the three battles of Jesus (days of the Lord) and the three days of Christ (rapture). The balance of the days of the Lord can be found in figure 25.

FIGURE 1: SECOND COMING OF JESUS EVENTS

Eschatological Jesus Event	Description	Chapter
Jerusalem: Visits and first campaign	Opened seal 5 Day 1 (Zech. 14:1–15)	7
First theophany First rapture of the church	Opened seal 7 (Matt. 24:27; Rev. 8:5)	3
Jehoshaphat: Second campaign	Blown trumpet 6 (Isa. 63:1, 5; Joel 3:2)	8
Second theophany Second rapture of church	Blown trumpet 7 (Rev. 11:19)	3
Armageddon: Third campaign	Poured bowl 6 (Rev. 19:11–16)	8
Third theophany	Poured bowl 7 (Rev. 16:18)	3

HARPAZÓ—SNATCHING AWAY THE SAINTS (RAPTURE)

Strong's Concordance defines the Greek verb *harpazó* as "to seize, catch up, snatch away."[3] It occurs fourteen times in the New Testament,[4] though

---

3   Strong, *Strong's Exhaustive Concordance*, s.v. "726 *harpazó*," accessed March 31, 2021, https://biblehub.com/greek/726.htm.

4   Matt. 11:12; 13:19; John 6:15; 10:12, 28, 29; Acts 8:39; 23:10; 2 Cor. 12:2, 4; 1 Thess. 4:17; Jude 1:23; Rev. 12:5.

the context is found in other parts of the Bible.[5] There are two Old Testament rapture-type scriptures, Genesis 5:24 with Enoch and 2 Kings 2:1, 11 with Elijah, though they do not contain the word *harpazó*. It is interesting to note that in Acts 8:39, Phillip was carried away horizontally from the Ethiopian eunuch to the town of Azotus. Similar to *harpazó* is the word *anabainó* in Revelation 11:11–12, when the two witnesses ascend into heaven.[6]

The word rapture comes from the concept of being seized or snatched away. In his book *Antichrist Before the Day of the Lord*, Dr. Alan Kurschner describes why the word rapture is appropriate.

> In the early church, one of the very first translations of the Bible was in Latin, and the translator chose *rapio* as the appropriate Latin verb to translate harpazó. Some have denied that the Bible teaches the rapture since the English term is not found in any English translations (even though the term "rapture" would be a very appropriate rendering for an English translation). This surface-level argument is not convincing since the concept of the rapture is clearly taught in I Thessalonians 4:17. The lack of the term itself is not unusual because many English theological terms are not found in the Bible while their concepts are found therein. Examples include the Trinity, monotheism, inspiration, omniscience, and scores of others.[7]

> Then we who are alive, who are left, will be *caught up* [*harpazó*] together with them in the clouds to meet the Lord in the air, and so we will always be with the Lord (1 Thess. 4:17, emphasis added).

OLIVET DISCOURSE

When Jesus was on the Mount of Olives, His disciples asked Him, "Tell us, when will these things be, and what will be the sign of your coming and of

---

5   Alan Kurschner, *Antichrist Before the Day of the Lord*, (Pompton Lakes, NJ: Eschatos Publishing, 2013), 82.

6   Strong, *Strong's Exhaustive Concordance*, s.v. "305 *anabainó*," accessed March 31, 2021, https://biblehub.com/greek/305.htm.

7   Kurschner, *Antichrist Before the Day of the Lord*, 82.

the end of the age?" (Matt. 24:3b). Jesus's response, recorded in Matthew 24–25, Mark 13, and Luke 21, is called the Olivet Discourse.

In Matthew 16:1–3, Jesus rebuked the Pharisees and Sadducees for not knowing the signs of the times yet still being able to tell the signs of the weather. Many church denominations and their congregations are at this moment asleep because they do not recognize the relationship of the Olivet Discourse to the coming (*parousia*) events of the seventieth week of Daniel, which includes the great tribulation of the fifth opened seal and the preceding tribulation of the fourth opened seal.

DISPENSATIONALISM AND PREMILLENNIALISM

John Nelson Darby, whose eschatology was adopted into the popular *Scofield Reference Bible* by Cyrus Scofield, is considered the father of dispensationalism, and he is credited with originating the pretribulation rapture theory.[8] Dispensationalists are premillennialists who assert that Revelation 20:6 refers to a future, literal thousand-year reign with Jesus Christ.[9] The premillennial view has five basic rapture positions:

1) Pretribulation, the most popular position, claims the rapture can happen at any moment prior to the beginning of the seventieth week of Daniel. The four movies and sixteen novels of the popular *Left Behind* series by Tim LaHaye and Jerry B. Jenkins are based on this pretribulation position.[10]

2) Midtribulation claims the rapture will happen on Day 1, in the middle of the seventieth week. This theory has lost favor over the last two or three decades.

3) Prewrath claims the rapture will happen during the second half of the seventieth week, after the great tribulation but before the wrath of God.

---

8   Wikipedia, s.v. "John Nelson Darby," accessed March 28, 2021, https://en.wikipedia.org/wiki/John_Nelson_Darby.
9   Wikipedia, s.v. "Dispensationalism," accessed March 28, 2021, https://en.wikipedia.org/wiki/Dispensationalism.
10   Wikipedia, s.v. *"Left Behind,"* accessed March 28, 2021, https://en.wikipedia.org/wiki/Left_Behind.

4) Beyond prewrath claims the rapture will happen during the second half of the seventieth week, after the great tribulation but before the (third) wrath of God. The earthly rapture is interpreted as being the unique theophany of Revelation 8:5 followed by the multitude rejoicing in heaven (Rev. 7:9–16).

5) Posttribulation claims the rapture will happen at the end of the seventieth week.

Figure 2 shows a representation of these historically accepted rapture positions, with each upward arrow representing the rapture. The prewrath and beyond prewrath raptures are shown in the figure as one upward arrow since their representative raptures of the elect are so close together chronologically.

FIGURE 2: FIVE RAPTURE POSITIONS

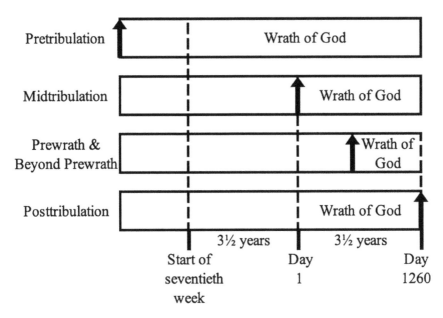

PREWRATH SUPPORTING REASONS AND PRETRIBULATION REBUTTALS

There are many scriptural reasons that support the Beyond Prewrath position over the pretribulation imminency rapture position. One of the most important reasons is its two back-to-back Scriptures: first the rapture with the first great eschatology theophany in Revelation 8:5 followed on the same day by the wrath of God in Revelation 8:6–7ff. A second and third great eschatological theophany in Revelation 11:19 and 16:18 add strength to this. Each of these great eschatology theophanies will later be shown as a unique Scriptural phrase of *peals of thunder, rumblings, flashes of lightning, and an earthquake.* Chapter 3 provides support for this new position.

According to 2 Thessalonians 2:2–5, the rebellion (falling away from faith) and the one who causes abomination must come before that day. This author equates this day with the first eschatological day of the Lord, identified as occurring on Day 1 in chapter 7 event 6 of this book. It will later be shown that the 2 Thessalonians 2:2–5 day of the Lord is not relative to the same day rapture (day of Christ) and the associated day of the Lord. In Daniel 9:27 the one who causes abomination on Day 1 "shall put an end to sacrifice and offering."

Proponents of the pretribulation position argue that the elect persevering through tribulation and then being raptured in Matthew 24 are for new believers. They refer to the multitude as "tribulation saints" who came to know Christ during the seventieth week of Daniel. Basically, they claim the Olivet Discourse applies to someone other than the church. Yet supporters of the pretribulation position are unable to point to a verse in Revelation 2 or 3 describing the church rapture with an eschatological theophany (as in Revelation 8:5, 11:19, and 16:18). There is no such verse before the apostle John arrives in heaven in Revelation 4:1. The pretribulation may quote Revelation 3:10 *open door* as being the rapture, though consider there is no rapture type theophany of "peals of thunder, rumblings, flashes of lightning, and an earthquake." Revelation 3:10 then seems to point to a different meaning. They also cannot explain the consequence of there not being an associated multitude in heaven rejoicing in Revelation 4, as there is in Revelation 7:9–17 and 19:1–5.[11] These are two significant new proofs against the pretribulation view.

Pretribulation infer that since the church is not discussed in Rev 4:1ff. when John arrives in heaven, therefore the church must have been raptured concurrently, if not before. Forming a position from only silence in Scripture should be considered nearly baseless. More importantly, if they were

---

11 For general information, a great resource is the free online video "7 Pretrib Problems and the Prewrath Rapture" on YouTube, https://www.youtube.com/watch?v=xwXoMNpOhos.

raptured when John arrived in heaven, then where is the multitude rejoicing in Revelation 4? There is no rejoicing and no reference to a multitude. The Beyond Prewrath Revelation 8:5 earthly rapture has their multitude rejoicing in Revelation 7:9–17.

Pretribulation proponents point to 1 Thessalonians 5:9, which states that the church is not destined to undergo the wrath of God, which all premillennial views agree on. The pretribulation view considers the entire seventieth week to be the wrath of God, so the church must be removed from the earth before this occurs. Yet, Matthew 24:21–22 clearly points to the elect (church) undergoing the great tribulation prior to the rapture. Analogous to this is Revelation 13:7a: "Also it [the beast of the sea] was allowed to make war on the saints and to conquer them." This eschatological event starts on Day 1.

> For then there will be great tribulation, such as has not been from the beginning of the world until now, no, and never will be. And if those days had not been cut short, no human being would be saved. But for the sake of the elect those days will be cut short. (Matt. 24:21–22)

TWENTY–FOUR ELDERS ARE NOT THE CHURCH AND/OR ISRAEL

Charles C. Ryrie says in his book *Revelation* that most premillennial writers have the twenty–four elders in Revelation 4:10 as the twenty–four redeemed individuals who represent all the redeemed.[12] Their pretribulation redeemed are claimed to be raptured when John arrives in heaven (Rev. 4:1ff). If so, they would need to be raptured before the start of the seventieth week of Daniel (Dan. 9:27 and Rev. 6).

There are seven reasons against this interpretation, where the first and second were discussed in the previous paragraph. Third, consider that Revelation 7:9 says a great multitude stands before the throne. Verse 10 says God "sits on the throne." Verse 11 says "And all the angels were standing around the throne and around the elders and the four living creatures." The great multitude in v. 9 and the elders in v. 11 are discussed separately. Also, in v. 13, the one elder discusses with John that the multitude who just arrived

---

12 Charles C. Ryrie, Revelation Everyday Bible Commentary, Moody Publishers, 820 N. LaSalle Blvd., Chicago, IL 60610, © 1996, 52.

in heaven are the ones from the great tribulation—again enforcing the thought that the elders and the multitude are different. This same distinction is shown in the second multitude rejoicing in heaven (Rev. 19:1–5). Since they are mentioned separately, the logical reasoning seems to mean they are not the same.

Fourth, 2 Thessalonians 2:1–5 has two events which must happen before the elect are gathered together (raptured). These two events—the rebellion and revealing of the man of lawlessness—must occur before the eschatological day of the Lord, supported as Day 1 (middle of the seventieth week). These two events prevent the redeemed being raptured earlier in Revelation 4.

Fifth, Beyond Prewrath has the church and Israel raptured separately, specifically, in Revelation 8:5 (end of first septet) and 11:19 (end of second septet). See chapters 2 and 8.

Sixth, the pretribulation may use Revelation 21:12, which describes Israel as the twelve gates, and v. 14, with the twelve foundations representing the church of twelve; though nowhere in these verses is the word "elder" equated to this.

Seventh, Revelation 2–3 represents seven and not twelve churches.

SEVENTIETH WEEK OF DANIEL VERSUS "THE TRIBULATION"

The seventieth week of Daniel (Dan. 9:27) is the last prophetic week of Daniel, which all premillennial scholars agree with. Unfortunately, it has become a tradition to also call this "the tribulation." The pretribulation position uses this phrase the most to represent a general sense of worldwide calamity against both their "tribulation saints" and the wicked. Supporting reasons against using this tradition are:

1) Jesus said his followers, "the elect," must endure tribulation (Matt. 24:21–22). There is no scripture that says the wicked will endure the tribulation. In Matthew 24:29–31, we see the tribulation ending before the coming of the Son of Man (rapture of the elect). There are at least three events during the seventieth week of Daniel when there is no tribulation.

   The first two are the sixth and seventh seals, which have no tribulation. The issue with the pretribulation phrase is that the beyond prewrath position has the tribulation of saints ending when the sixth seal is opened (Matt. 24:29), continuing into the seventh opened seal, and then the rapture. Since these opened seals have no tribulation for the elect within the seventieth week of Daniel, then the entire prophetic week should not be called the tribulation.

The third reason is the opened seals one to three are described as "birth pains." If they were meant to be about the tribulation, then the apostle Paul would have labeled them that way—as corresponding with apostle John's parallel fourth and fifth opened seals (Matt. 24:9, 21).

2) The *Scofield Reference Bible* of 1909 is when the pretribulation started to become a very popular premillennial view in the United States. Nowhere within this historic pretribulation commentary by Cyrus Scofield does the phrase "the tribulation" appear to be mentioned. Considering the frequency of current pretribulation scholars referring to the tribulation, it should give them pause as to why Cyrus Scofield did not include this phrase in his commentary.

3) All of the different premillennial positions should be looking for ways to come to agreement. This phrase change from "the tribulation" to "the seventieth week of Daniel" is a simple way to accomplish this. "For God has not destined us (*believers*) for (*the*) wrath (*of God*), but to obtain salvation through our Lord Jesus Christ" (1 Thess. 5:9, emphasis added).

FALLING AWAY

We've seen that 2 Thessalonians 2:3 describes a rebellion, or falling away, before the eschatological day of the Lord. Jesus defines this falling away in the parable of the sower: "As for what was sown on rocky ground, this is the one who hears the word and immediately receives it with joy, yet he has no root in himself, but endures for a while, and when tribulation or persecution arises on account of the word, immediately he falls away" (Matt. 13:20–21). The tribulation, followed by the great tribulation, will be a historic time of persecution for those who do not take the mark of the beast and worship its image. Our faith should grow strong now regardless of whether this persecution occurs in our lifetimes or not.

SIXTY-NINE WEEKS OF DANIEL

Daniel wrote his prophecy of seventy weeks in the sixth century BC. Later the prophecy began with the decree from King Artaxerxes for Nehemiah to build a second temple in Jerusalem (Neh. 2:5). Daniel 9:25–26 predicted it would take seven prophetic weeks to build the temple. Then after sixty-two prophetic weeks, the Anointed One would be cut off. The Anointed One is Jesus being crucified and not having His kingdom, at least not until the end of the seventieth week of Daniel. Since Jesus was cut-off, Daniel's time clock has stopped. So, a total of sixty-nine prophetic weeks have elapsed in history, with one prophetic week equaling seven literal Hebrew years.

In his 1895 book *The Coming Prince*, Sir Robert Anderson calculated that one Hebrew year equals 360 days.[13] One month equals thirty days, and one year equals twelve months (Gen. 7:11; 8:3; Rev. 12:6; 13:5). We are now waiting for the start of the seventieth week of Daniel, which begins with the multi-national seven Hebrew year treaty with Israel.

DURATION OF THE SECOND HALF OF DANIEL'S SEVENTIETH WEEK

The second half of the seventieth prophetic week of Daniel is described in both the Old and New Testament prophecies in different time units, which scholars agree all have the same duration. Revelation 11:2–3 has the same duration though the event of witnesses arriving is before and not on Day 1 since they leave in the sixth blown trumpet, which is before Day 1,260.

1) Time, times, and half a time (Dan. 7:25, 12:7; Rev. 12:14)

2) 1,260 days (Rev. 12:6; cf. Rev. 11:3)

3) Forty–two months (Rev. 13:5; cf. Rev. 11:2)

4) Second half of the week (Dan. 9:27)

Knowing these different described time units are the same allows prophetic scriptures to be associated to understand its meaning. These scriptures describe a period when both the saints (church) and the Jews will have massive persecution. Day 1 of this time period begins with "on the

---

13   Robert Anderson, *The Coming Prince*, (Grand Rapids: Kregel, 1972), iii.

wing of abominations shall come one who makes desolate" at a future new temple expected to be built in Jerusalem on the Temple Mount (Dan. 9:27).

The church will not live through the entire 1,260 days on earth since the persecution of our faith will be cut short when we are saved with a physical rapture.

> And if those days had not been cut short, no human being would be saved. But for the sake of the *elect* [church] those days will be *cut short*. (Matt. 24:22, emphasis added)

GENTILE GRAFTING MYSTERY

"This mystery is that the Gentiles are fellow heirs, members of the same body, and partakers of the promise in Christ Jesus through the gospel" (Eph. 3:6). Therefore, the prophetic Scriptures have an application to everyone, both Jews and Gentiles.

ANTICHRIST

There are two types of antichrist. A general type of antichrist is "he who denies the Father and the Son" (1 John 2:22b). This type of antichrist has been around since before the birth of Jesus. The second type is specific and has an eschatological significance (1 John 2:18). This second type of specific antichrist will be denoted as the Antichrist.

Matthew 24:15 describes the "abomination of desolation" standing in the holy place. Standing indicates he will have physical form and 2 Thessalonians 2:3–4 refers to him as a human, "the man of lawlessness" and "the son of destruction." This man of lawlessness was previously known as the little horn in Daniel 8:9 before he gave up his goat horn. "And the goat is the king of Greece" (Dan. 8:21a). The apostle John saw "a beast rising out of the sea with ten horns and seven heads, with ten diadems on its horns and blasphemous names on its heads" (Rev. 13:1). This beast parallels the ten horns of Revelation 12:3 (dragon) and Daniel 7:24 (little horn). This beast rising out of the sea is considered the empowered (by Satan) eschatological son of destruction who "is an eighth" from Revelation 17:11. The first son of destruction was Judas Iscariot in John 17:12, who Satan also indwelt within (Luke 22:3; John 13:27).

On Day 1, Satan—a spirit being—is expected to enter the man of lawlessness. Once they become one as the Antichrist, the man of lawlessness would be expected to be revealed (2 Thess. 2:3–5) and the temple abomination of desolation to occur (Dan. 9:27, Matt. 24:15), which begins the great tribulation (Matt. 24:22, Rev. 6:9–11). A few years later, this human beast will be captured and thrown alive into the lake of fire by Jesus during the Armageddon campaign (the sixth poured bowl in Rev. 19:20). The spirit of the Antichrist, who is Satan, will be captured, held in the bottomless pit on a chain, and then released a thousand years later (Rev. 20:1–3). After the thousand years, Satan will be released and will again deceive the earth (Rev. 20:7–8). At the end of the millennium, he will be thrown into the lake of fire (Rev. 20:7–10).

Chapter 2

New Understandings

JOEL 2:28–32 IS IN THE SIXTH TRUMPET

Almost all scholars interpret Joel 2:28–32 and Acts 2:17–21 as occurring during the sixth opened seal, often called the "wrath of the Lamb." Scholars apparently associate the wrath of the Lamb of Revelation 6:16–17 with Acts 2:19 and Joel 2:30, where darkness, blood, and fire are mentioned. However, nowhere when the sixth opened seal is broken in Revelation 6:12–17 are blood and fire mentioned. We only find all three in the Jehoshaphat campaign, part of the sixth blown trumpet.[1] The "wrath of the Lamb" (second day of Lord) should be considered the perspective of those with the mark of the beast, but for believers it will be a time to rejoice since it marks the end of the great tribulation (Matt. 24:29). Chapter 8 discusses the Jehoshaphat campaign in more detail.

FIGURE 3: DARKNESS, BLOOD, AND FIRE

Event	Darkness?	Blood?	Fire?
Day 1	Mixed	Yes	Yes
	Zech. 14:6	Ezek. 38:21–22	Ezek. 38:22
Opened seal 6	Yes	No	No
	Rev. 6:12		
Blown trumpet 1	No	Yes	Yes
		Rev. 8:7	Rev. 8:7
Blown trumpet 2	No	Yes	Yes
		Rev. 8:8	Rev. 8:8

---

1   See figures 3 and 24, as well as chapter 8 for more details. The seventh opened seal, seventh blown trumpet, first poured bowl, and seventh poured bowl were not included in figure 3 since there is no blood, fire, or darkness in any of them.

FIGURE 3 (*continued*)

Event	Darkness?	Blood?	Fire?
Blown trumpet 3	No	Yes	Yes
		Rev. 8:10	Rev. 8:10
Blown trumpet 4	No[2]	No	No
	Rev. 8:12		
Blown trumpet 5	Yes	No	No
	Rev. 9:2	Rev. 9:5	
Blown trumpet 6	**Yes**[3]	**Yes**	**Yes**
	Rev. 14:18–19	Rev. 9:18	Rev. 9:18
Poured bowl 2	No	Yes	No
		Rev. 16:3	
Poured bowl 3	No	Yes	No
		Rev. 16:4	
Poured bowl 4	No	No	Yes
			Rev. 16:8
Poured bowl 5	Yes	No	No
	Rev. 16:10		
Poured bowl 6	No	Yes	No
		Rev. 19:15	

Finally, the recipients of the spiritual salvation of Acts 2:17–21 appear to be only the Jewish people. In Acts 2:17, three times the recipient group is addressed as "your" people. Since Peter was Jewish by birth, these prophecies of Joel appear to apply only to the Jewish people. The Jewish people are saved a day before "the great and awesome day of the LORD." This day of the Lord is considered by this author to be the Jehoshaphat campaign (Joel 2:31–32a), part of the sixth blown trumpet. After the seventh blown trumpet

2   See chapter 4 for discussion of why Rev. 8:12 is not defined as darkness.
3   See chapter 8 with Jehoshaphat campaign.

sounds, they are raptured as the elect (church) in the second great theophany of Revelation 11:19. We know they missed the first great theophany rapture since the Jewish tribes wail on account of Him in Revelation 1:7.

The reference to blood in Acts 2:19 is interpreted as death and not from injury. This means the fifth blown trumpet does not have death. There will be blood from injury in Revelation 9:5 though Scripture says they will be unable to kill themselves (Rev. 9:6). Even if injury was interpreted as blood, it still does not change the outcome of figure 3 since there is no fire. Darkness, blood, and fire must all be present to show relevance to Acts 2:19.

NOT A ONE-WORLD GOVERNMENT

This author's new understanding is that there will not be a one-world government during the seventieth week of Daniel. Many have an understanding on a one world government likely based on Daniel 2:39: "Another kingdom inferior to you shall arise after you, and yet a third kingdom of bronze, which shall rule over all the earth." The third kingdom was the Grecian Empire, which we know from history never ruled over the entire earth. Therefore, the Bible is speaking in hyperbole.

A second supporting reason against the Antichrist conquering the world and having a one-world government is in Daniel 9:26, where the angel Gabriel declares to the prophet Daniel: "And to the end there shall be war. Desolations are decreed." If the Antichrist had conquered the world, then he would not be at war. So those countries at war with the Antichrist will still have their own governments.

TREATY VERSUS A PEACE TREATY

Many claim that the seventieth week of Daniel starts with a peace treaty. Both Daniel 9:27 and Isaiah 28:15 refer to a treaty, but nowhere in Scripture does it say that it will be a peace treaty. Scripturally, it should be looked at in the opposite perspective. It makes no sense for Daniel's seventieth week to be prophetically considered a peace treaty since no country would sign a "peace" treaty for a specified amount of time. It does not prevent the future prophecy of a seven–Daniel–year "death covenant" being labeled as a peace treaty. A peace treaty should be considered as saying "We will not make war against each other." Treaties can include such as trade agreements for agriculture, information technology, balance of trade, and selling land.

Another agreement could be to build infrastructure, such as roads, bridges, and tunnels.

> We have made a covenant with death, and with Sheol we have an agreement. (Isa. 28:15a)

> And he shall make a strong covenant with many for one week, and for half of the week he shall put an end to sacrifice and offering. And on the wing of abominations shall come one who makes desolate, until the decreed end is poured out on the desolator." (Dan. 9:27)

ANTICHRIST WILL MAKE THE COVENANT STRONG

A common misunderstanding is that the prince will make a covenant during the seventieth week of Daniel. Daniel 9:27 tells us the prince will make a strong covenant with many, though it does not say he will initiate it. Many translations say he will confirm a covenant., which again can not be interpreted as initiating it. Some say the covenant will be a private, unannounced treaty. This does not seem reasonable considering this covenant is between Israel and many other countries. This event would be expected to make international news.

The following supports Isaiah 28:14–29 being parallel to Daniel's seventieth week. Isaiah 28:14 addresses those Jerusalem leaders who signed the covenant. Verse 18 discusses how their covenant with death (Sheol) will be annulled. This appears to parallel Daniel 9:27 (emphasis added) with "He shall *make a strong covenant* with many for one week, and for half of the week he shall put an end to sacrifice and offering." Making the covenant strong could, for example, include providing a UN type of peacekeeping force or other logistical and financial types of support.

The prince who breaks the covenant (treaty) is identified earlier in Daniel 7:8 as the little horn. Many incorrectly identify this person as the Antichrist. It is not until later on Day 1 when he becomes the Antichrist. Isaiah 28:19 describes this broken covenant as bringing sheer terror to Israel.

In Isaiah 28:21, the Lord will be roused and rise up in anger, which is considered the first eschatological day of the Lord. Basically, the Lord will be attacking Gog. Since Gog provoked his anger in various ways, the Lord's attack should be considered a counterattack likely same–day Israel was attacked on Day 1 (see chapter 7, event 6).

ABSOLUTE DEATH OF A QUARTER OF THE EARTH IN THE SIXTH OPENED SEAL IS NOT SCRIPTURAL

Another popular understanding of Scripture is that one quarter of the earth's population will be killed—a physical first death. This is based on the fourth opened seal in Revelation 6:7–8, where a rider named Death sitting on a pale horse is given authority to kill over a fourth of the earth. An assumption is being made that this authority will mean the death of a quarter of the earth. However, having the authority to do something does not necessarily equate to this occurring.

If the rider Death did kill a fourth of the earth that he had authority over, how could the later-empowered man of lawlessness (Antichrist) have a military force at war with other countries until the end? "Its end shall come with a flood, and to the end there shall be war. Desolations are decreed" (Dan. 9:26b). We see wars will continue by the prince and the people till the end. Chapter 9 will show that the prince is the Antichrist and the people of the prince are the ten kings. If they are still at war till the end, then it is not logical that he would kill the quarter of the earth he has authority over. Otherwise, they would have no military force among that quarter of the earth to be at war with the other three-quarters of the earth. Besides, Satan's goal is for a second everlasting death in the lake of fire. Satan will accomplish this "if anyone worships the beast and its image and receives a mark on his forehead or on his hand" (Rev. 14:9a).

It is certainly possible with his given authority to kill a quarter of the earth. He can only accomplish this by killing some of those he does not have authority over and, if desired, some of those he does have authority over. For example, he could kill half of the quarter of the earth he has authority over (total of an eighth) and a sixth of those he does not have authority over (total of an eighth). The total would be a quarter of the earth. We know from scripture that he will *deal* with the strongest of fortresses, which are likely those he does not have authority. Dealing with does not necessarily equate to those being killed. It could have to do with restrictions in trade to those countries.

> He shall *deal* with the strongest fortresses with the help of a foreign god. (Daniel 11:39a, emphasis added)

TWO WITNESSES ARRIVE BEFORE DAY 1

The two witnesses of Revelation 11 will arrive just prior to Day 1, not on Day 1. The following four events of the witnesses help in unraveling this. These supporting reasons point to the two witnesses leaving earth on Day 1,259 after being on earth for at least 1,263.5 days. Therefore, the two witnesses must arrive several days before Day 1. This position is based on the third septet of poured bowls as being thirty days and after the seventieth week of Daniel, that is Days 1,261 to 1,290 (Dan. 12:11).

First, they leave earth at the end of the sixth blown trumpet (Rev. 11:12). "And at that hour there was a great earthquake, and a tenth of the city fell. Seven thousand people were killed in the earthquake" (Rev. 11:13a). This last Scripture verse of the sixth blown trumpet occurred at the hour the two witnesses were taken to heaven. Therefore, it seems reasonable they left earth on the last day of the sixth blown trumpet. After the sixth blown trumpet, there is one more blown trumpet remaining, the seventh blown trumpet, thought to be on Day 1,260.[4] This points to the sixth blown trumpet possibly ending on Day 1,259.

Second, the two witnesses are on earth for at least 1,263.5 days. That is, they prophesy for 1,260 days (three and a half years of Daniel) in Revelation 11:3. They are dead for three and a half days in Revelation 11:9–10. Plus, there is a relatively short, unknown amount of time on earth before they are called up to heaven in Revelation 11:11–12.

Third, the Lord says in Malachi 4:5, "Behold, I will send you Elijah the prophet before the great and awesome day of the LORD comes." Elijah would be one of the two witnesses described in Revelation 11. The earliest eschatological day of the Lord is on Day 1, also called the Jerusalem campaign.

Fourth, the second half of the seventieth week of Daniel is 1,260 days long (Rev. 12:6; Dan. 9:27).

1 THESSALONIANS 5:2–3 APPLIES TO THE WICKED

A few scholars apply the 1 Thessalonians 5:2–3 prophecy to Israel on Day 1 as the start of Jacob's trouble. Instead, it should be applied to a different

---

4   This one-day event is discussed further in chapter 8.

group of people on the same-day rapture in Revelation 8:5 and the wrath of God in Revelation 8:6ff.

First, 1 Thessalonians 5:3 says "they will not escape." These scholars' prophetic interpretation disagrees with Revelation 12:13–16, which says some of Israel will escape and be protected and nourished for 1,260 days.

Second, the "people" referred to in 1 Thessalonians 5:3 are the individuals who say there is peace and security. They are not the brothers (*adelphos*) in 1 Thessalonians 5:4. *Strong's Concordance* explains that the word "brother" (*adelphos*) is used to mean "a brother, member of the same religious community, especially a fellow Christian."[5] Therefore, this appears to say that Christian brothers will not be surprised, though the people (those with the mark of the beast) will be. These reasons point to the prophecy being applied to the wicked, those with the mark of the beast, who worship his image.

> Now concerning the times and the seasons, brothers, you have no need to have anything written to you. For you yourselves are fully aware that the day of the Lord will come like a thief in the night. While people are saying, "There is peace and security," then sudden destruction will come upon them as labor pains come upon a pregnant woman, and they will not escape. *But you are not in darkness, brothers [adelphoi], for that day to surprise you like a thief.* For you are all children of light, children of the day. We are not of the night or of the darkness. (1 Thess. 5:1–5, emphasis added)

2 THESSALONIANS 2:1–5 ESCHATOLOGICAL DAY OF THE LORD DOES NOT APPLY TO THE SAME–DAY RAPTURE

Many premillennial scholars have 2 Thessalonians 2:2–5 day of the Lord chronologically associated with the day of the Lord of Matthew 24:36–41 and its same–day rapture of Matthew 24:29–31. There are five reasons against this interpretation:

First, scholars are interpreting from scripture that Paul and his believers are contemplating they may have entered the eschatological day of the Lord

---

5   James Strong, *Strong's Exhaustive Concordance of the Bible*, Bible Hub, s.v. "80 *adelphos*," accessed April 1, 2021, https://biblehub.com/greek/80.htm.

and therefore missed the same day rapture, which is unreasonable. Though how can they enter this day of the Lord if they are to be raptured for their faith before the day of the Lord? The only apparent solution to understand this is to have a separate and earlier eschatological day of the Lord. Basically, scripture seems to be directing us to at least two separate eschatological days of the Lord.

If scholars' understanding of 2 Thessalonians 2:2–5 eschatological day of the Lord had occurred, it would mean the apostle Paul and those asking the question would have missed the rapture. The thought of this having any truth is completely unjustified. This is the same Paul whose aprons or handkerchiefs healed the sick (Acts 19:11–12) and brought back to life the young man who fell from a third story window (Acts 20:9–12).

Second, Paul does not say (in 2 Thess. 2:2–4) that they (believers) will not enter that day of the Lord. He is saying for believers to not be alarmed, for that day will not come until the two events in 2 Thessalonians 2:2–5 occur first. Therefore, Paul expects the church to enter this eschatological day of the Lord sometime in the future.

Third, chapter 7 event 6 describes an earlier eschatological day of the Lord (in Zech. 14:1–12) of physical death in Israel, which is probably on Day 1. So, this could be the earlier day of the Lord that Paul has in mind.

Fourth, one of the two prerequisites of this day of the Lord would be the revealing of the man of lawlessness (2 Thess. 2:2–5). Him being revealed could represent when the historic abomination of desolation occurs in the Jerusalem temple (Dan. 9:27). Since they were located about 800 miles away in Corinth during Paul's second missionary journey, and news traveled slowly back then, it seems they wanted to know right then rather than to wait several weeks or months.

Paul assured them that two events (in 2 Thess. 2:2–3) must occur prior to the (apparent first) eschatological day of the Lord. So, their concern in asking Paul the question then appears to be whether their current tribulation (2 Cor. 11:24–28; Acts 13:48–52; 14:5–6) would lead to the eschatological great tribulation of Matthew 24:15–26.

In conclusion, the eschatological day of the Lord in 2 Thessalonians 2:2–5 seems to be a reference to an earlier day of the Lord and not the later day of the Lord of Matthew 24:36–41 with its same–day rapture. This earlier day of the Lord is likely on Day 1, as described in chapter 7.

Now concerning the coming of our Lord Jesus Christ and our being gathered together to him [rapture], we ask you, brothers, not to be quickly shaken in mind or alarmed, either by a spirit or a spoken word, or a letter seeming to be from us, to the effect that the [first] *day of the Lord* [Day 1] has come. Let no one deceive you in any way. For that day will not come, unless the rebellion comes first, and the man of lawlessness is revealed, the son of destruction, who opposes and exalts himself against every so–called god or object of worship, so that he takes his seat in the temple of God, proclaiming himself to be God. (2 Thess. 2:1–4, emphasis added)

THE ANTICHRIST DOES NOT EXIST AT THE START OF THE SEVENTIETH WEEK

We know from Daniel 9:27 that *he* will make the seven–year covenant *strong*. It has become a tradition to call the person making the covenant strong the Antichrist. Earlier, Daniel 8:9–12 describes this person as the "little horn." The well–known *New Scofield Study Bible* pretribulation position commentary also identifies him as the little horn and not the Antichrist.[6]

CONCLUSION

Many scholars interpret 2 Thessalonians 2:2–5 that Paul may enter the day of the Lord and therefore miss the rapture. For an apostle to miss the rapture is an unreasonable interpretation. A better interpretation would be that they are describing a separate and earlier eschatological day of the Lord.

One of the most prevalent misconceptions in the church today concerns the signs of Joel 2:28–32 relating to the sixth opened seal. The only eschatology event that has darkness, blood, and fire is the Jehoshaphat campaign of the sixth blown trumpet (Rev. 9:2, 18; 14:18–19). The dramatic eschatological implications of this understanding of Scripture cannot be understated. It will provide support in changing when the rapture of the

---

6   New Scofield Study Bible, by Oxford University Press, Inc., © 1967, Daniel 9:27 foot note (7), 1207.

church is thought to occur. The next chapter identifies exactly where in Scripture this author thinks the rapture should occur.[7]

---

7   Chapter 5 supports the position that the Antichrist does not come into existence until Day 1.

Chapter 3

Seventh Opened Seal and Silence in Heaven

PURPOSE

Current prewrath scholarly interpretation has the rapture of the church occurring chronologically between the sixth opened seal (Rev. 6:12) and the seventh opened seal (Rev. 8:1). This book presents a different view, with the rapture (*parousia*) in Matthew 24:27 occurring with the lightning (*astrapē*) in Revelation 8:5. First, we will see that Scripture is not always written chronologically. This insight will help in understanding that the sealing of the 144,000 and the great multitude in heaven (Rev. 7) is the consequence of the theophany rapture in Revelation 8:5. Second, the rapture of the church will occur on either the seventh or eighth day when opening the seventh seal, based on Jesus's analogy to Noah. Third, this author will identify three associated unique great theophany phrases in Revelation 8:5; 11:19; and 16:18, which all have eschatological rapture implications. Fourth, this author will present strong evidence for a rapture occurring in Revelation 8:5 followed by the wrath of God in Revelation 8:6–7ff. based on Jesus analogy to Noah and Lot (Luke 17:22–30).

ALL SCRIPTURE IS NOT CHRONOLOGICAL

The position of this book is that the presence of the multitude in heaven (Rev. 7:9–17) is a consequence of the rapture in Revelation 8:5. Scripture is not always written in chronological order, as the following three examples show:

1) Jeremiah 46–47 was written about 609 BC, but Jeremiah 21–45 was written later, in about 588 BC. Yet Jeremiah 46–47 is numbered after Jeremiah 21–45.[1]

---

1   "Jeremiah," in Bible Timeline, Bible Hub, 2010, https://biblehub.com/timeline/jeremiah/1.htm.

2) Daniel is written in two chiastic structures, which are poetic. The first poetic structure is Daniel 2:4 to 7:28, and the second is all of Daniel 8 to 12. This points to all of Daniel chapters as not being understood as being chronological. Daniel 2 to 5:30 has the king as Belshazzar, though his succeeding son dies in Daniel 5:30. Then there is the reign of Darius and Cyrus in Daniel 5:30 to 6:28. Later in Daniel 7:1, King Belshazzar becomes king again, though he died in Daniel 5. Later in Daniel 9, 10, and 11, Darius and Cyrus come back.

3) Ezekiel 29:17 occurred during the twenty-seventh year of Babylonian exile. Later verses in Ezekiel were chronologically earlier, including Ezekiel 30:20 (eleventh year), 31:1 (eleventh year), 32:1 (twelfth year), 32:17 (twelfth year), 33:21 (twelfth year), and 40:1 (twenty-fifth year).

RAPTURE AND WRATH ON SAME DAY

Following the prewrath rapture position discussed in chapter 1, the rapture occurs on the same day the wrath of God begins. "Just as it was in the days of Noah, so will it be in the days of the Son of Man. They were eating and drinking and marrying and being given in marriage, until the day when Noah entered the ark, and the flood came and destroyed them all" (Luke 17:26–27). Genesis 7:12–13 says Noah's family entered the ark and was saved while the flood destroyed the world. Therefore, Jesus's analogy indicates that the righteous will be physically protected while the unrighteous will receive the wrath of God on the same day. The removal of Noah's righteous family during the flood is indicative of the coming rapture and wrath of God. Jesus also made the analogy to Lot and his family who escaped by leaving the same day of the destruction of the wicked (Luke 17:28–29).

EXISTING VERSUS PROPOSED BEYOND PREWRATH

The existing prewrath position was proposed about thirty years ago by Robert Van Kampen in his book *The Sign* and Marvin Rosenthal in his book *The Pre-wrath Rapture of the Church*.[2] They suggest the rapture occurs in Revelation 7:9–17 with the multitude rejoicing in heaven. They

---

2   Marvin Rosenthal, *The Pre-wrath Rapture of the Church* (Nashville: Thomas Nelson, 1990); Robert Van Kampen, *The Sign* (Wheaton, IL: Crossway Books, 1992).

use a chronological interpretation of Revelation 6–8. This author proposes a different chronological sequence: Revelation 6, Revelation 8:1–5 (with the rapture in v. 5), Revelation 7, and finally Revelation 8:6ff. (the wrath of God with the trumpets and bowls). Moving the chronological order of Scripture seems to be allowed since Revelation 7 is not identified as occurring during either the sixth or seventh opened seal.

The existing prewrath has the wrath of God occurring in Revelation 8:1ff., starting with "silence in heaven," though there is no other Scripture with these exact words to help support verse 1 as the wrath of God. Verse 1 by its description does not appear to be representative of a wrath of God event and therefore forces the existing prewrath position to look in verse 2ff. for the wrath of God. Only when we look at "hail and fire, mixed with blood" (v. 7) is there a match to the "fire and sulfur" of the days of Lot (Luke 17:28–29). This author uses Daniel's prophetic time ratio of 360:1 to equate the half an hour duration of heaven in Revelation 8:1 to seven and a half literal days on earth. Since this author's interpretation of verse 1 is then longer than one literal day, it prevents their rapture (Rev. 7:9–17) occuring before the later wrath of God in Revelation 8:2ff. If these calculations are correct, then trying to interpret these Scriptures chronologically would not be allowed.

Therefore, Revelation 8:7 is part of the wrath of God and the rapture cannot happen before Revelation 8:1, then we must look for a rapture event during the seventh opened seal in verses 2–5. Verse 5 describes a theophany of "peals of thunder, rumblings, flashes of lightning, and an earthquake" that takes place during what this author calls the first great eschatology theophany, since the same eschatological theophany can only be found in Revelation 11:19 and 16:18. These three theophany Scriptures will be shown to each describe eschatological rapture event, which adds significant strength to the idea that Revelation 8:5 describes a rapture of the elect. This author considers Revelation 7, where the 144,000 are sealed on earth and the great multitude in heaven rejoices after arriving from the great tribulation, to be a consequence of the rapture in 8:5. These back-to-back Scriptures in Revelation 8:5–7 form strong evidence for the proposed Beyond Prewrath position. If Revelation 8:5 is the rapture, then verses 1–4 in the opened seventh seal can be deduced to represent light, as discussed several paragraphs later.

Lastly, in Revelation 7:10 we see the multitude in heaven "crying out with a loud voice." If the events in Revelation 6–8 occur in chronological order, how would it be possible for this multitude a few verses later in Revelation 8:1 to have silence in heaven for about half an hour? Those in heaven from the rapture are "clothed in white robes, with palm branches in their hands" (Rev. 7:9b). It does not seem possible that a multitude in heaven with physical bodies holding palm branches would be able to remain silent for half an hour. Just one person dropping a palm branch would make a noise.

SEVENTH SEAL CONCEPTUAL TIMELINE

Figure 4 provides a conceptual timeline around the seventh opened seal based on the rapture occurring in Revelation 8:5 (the end of the seventh opened seal), with the wrath of God in Revelation 8:7ff. (blown trumpets and poured bowls) occurring on the same day. This will be used in analyzing each time component.

FIGURE 4: SEVENTH OPENED SEAL CONCEPTUAL TIMELINE

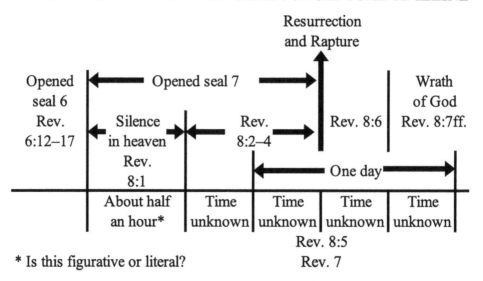

THREE SEPTETS: EACH WITH A RAPTURE AND DO NOT OVERLAP

Some say the seventh opened seal overlaps with the blown trumpets. The following provides support against this.

A septet is a group of seven similar things. In Revelation, there are three septets for the opened seals, blown trumpets, and poured bowls. At the end of each septet, there is the repeated scriptural pattern of peals of thunder, rumblings, flashes of lightning, and an earthquake. Each appears to be associated with a rapture: first rapture (church), second rapture (Israel), and third rapture (sheep being righteous); that is, seventh opened seal (Rev. 8:5), seventh blown trumpet (Rev. 11:19), and seventh poured bowl (Rev. 16:18), respectively.

There are three other shorter phrases which do not contain "earthquake". The first is Revelation 4:5 when John is in the presence of God on the throne. The second is Revelation 14:2, with the 144,000 on Mt. Zion. The third is Revelation 19:6 with the multitude at the marriage supper of the Lamb. This would make six of these phrases with thunder. Seven were expected since in Revelation 10:3 there are seven thunders which sounded. Ezekiel 43:2 with rushing waters could be the seventh with lightning equivalent since it is associated with His voice (Rev. 1:15).

The conceptual figure 4 points to the seventh opened seal not overlapping the first blown trumpet. This concept is built on Luke 17:22–30, which has the eschatological return of the son of man "as it was during Noah and Lot." We know from Lot that the righteous were saved (fled on foot from Sodom) on the same day, before the wrath of God against the wicked. From Noah, we see the Lord shut the door of the ark on the same day the floods came and destroyed the wicked. These same–day events are representative of the rapture (Rev. 8:5, end of first septet) and the start of the first blown trumpet (Rev. 8:6–7, start of the second septet).

Another example against this overlapping theory uses the fifth opened seal, fifth blown trumpet, and fifth poured bowl. The fifth opened seal and fifth poured bowl do not have darkness, though the fifth blown trumpet (in Rev. 9:5) does. The darkness column in figure 3 in chapter 2 shows other disproving examples against this theory.

Therefore, it seems the future prophetic prophecy of Luke 17:22–30 forces the first and second septets to not overlap.

REVELATION 8:1: SILENCE IN HEAVEN

This analysis will continue by looking at the seventh opened seal of Revelation 8:1–5 verse by verse, followed by the trumpets issued in Revelation 8:6 and then the wrath of God in Revelation 8:7ff.

> When the Lamb opened the seventh seal, there was silence in heaven for about half an hour. (Rev. 8:1)

The analogy Jesus made about Noah and the flood in Luke 17:26 may be more than just a reference to the rapture and wrath of God occurring on the same day. "And Noah and his sons and his wife and his sons' wives with him went into the ark to escape the waters of the flood. Of clean animals, and of animals that are not clean, and of birds, and of everything that creeps on the ground, two and two, male and female, went into the ark with Noah, as God had commanded Noah. And after seven days the waters of the flood came upon the earth" (Gen. 7:7–10). After this, "on the very same day" (Gen. 7:13a), Noah and his seven crew-family members "entered the ark" (Gen. 7:13c). These Scriptures appear to mean that Noah needed seven literal days to fulfill the Lord's commandment, given the massive effort required to load, likely cage, and then begin feeding and watering each animal over the three floors in the ark.

Could the seven-literal-day duration before the flood (wrath of God) be analogous to the duration of the seventh open seal of Revelation 8:1–5 before the eschatological wrath of God in Revelation 8:6-7ff? That is, could the eschatological "silence in heaven for about half an hour" in Revelation 8:1 have a corresponding length of time on earth as with Noah? To convert from heaven to earth time, we will use Daniel's prophetic-to-literal time ratio to see if it has merit. Since Daniel's prophecy of sixty-nine weeks was fulfilled, we know that one prophetic week equals seven Daniel years. The duration of the silence in heaven then becomes about seven and a half days, as calculated in figure 5. The ratio of seven and a half days to half an hour is a prophetic time ratio of 360:1. Therefore, the idea of Jesus's analogy to Noah conveying a second meaning seems to have merit, which will be examined in more detail.

FIGURE 5: SILENCE IN HEAVEN CALCULATED

(About 0.5 hour in heaven) / 1 week = (Literal time) / 7 years

Given Daniel's prophetic ratio of one week equals seven literal years and keeping in mind that one Hebrew year is 360 days, we can calculate the equivalent literal time on earth.

Literal time = (About 0.5 hour) x 7 years / 1 week

Next, we multiple by ratios of equality to solve the equation.

Literal time = (About 0.5 hour) x (7 years x (360 days/1 year)) / (1 week x (168 hours/1 week))

Literal time = (About 0.5 hour) x 2520 days / 168 hours

Literal time = About 7.5 days

REVELATION 8:2: TRUMPETS GIVEN (READY)

In Revelation 8:2 seven angels are given seven trumpets for the coming wrath of God, though they are not told to blow them yet. So the wrath of God has not yet started. A good memory association to use with this Scripture is an analogy to an old military command given to soldiers with weapons: (1) "ready" (Rev. 8:2), (2) "aim" (Rev. 8:6), and (3) "fire" (Rev. 8:7ff.). The church is expected to be on earth when the "ready" command is issued in heaven, though we will be in heaven when the "aim" and "fire" commands are issued to the angels for those remaining on earth.

> Then I saw the seven angels who stand before God, and seven trumpets were given to them ["ready"]. (Rev. 8:2)

REVELATION 8:3–4: INCENSE

In Leviticus 16:13, God commanded the priest to burn sweet incense to prevent him from dying when entering the holy of holies. There appears to be a similar analogy being made with Revelation 8:3–4 for Christians not to die before entering heaven.

SEVENTH OPENED SEAL: RAPTURE ON SEVENTH OR EIGHTH DAY

Previously we converted the duration of the silence in heaven in Revelation 8:1 to seven and a half literal days on earth. Revelation 8:5 is the last verse-event of the seventh opened seal (Rev. 8:1–5). Therefore, when the darkness of the sixth opened seal (Rev. 6:12) ends and we enter the expected light of the seventh opened seal, we would expect the analogous duration of Noah days. The expected light of the seventh opened seal is seen in Luke 17:26–28, where Jesus describes people planting and building before the wrath of God.

In Genesis 7:4 these seven days were an exact amount of time and not figurative. The Revelation 8:2–4 duration is interpreted as being much less than seven and a half days since it was not mentioned in Scripture. Therefore, this author assumes the duration will not exceed about one day. The duration of the Revelation 8:5 rapture event must be a short amount of time considering the well-known rapture of Elijan's chariots of fire in 2 Kings 2:11. Since Jesus's analogy in Luke 17:26 referred to Noah in Genesis 7:4, the seven-day duration provides a good match to the Revelation 8:1–5 duration. The first inclination that I had is to place the rapture on the seventh day after the opening of the seventh seal. But we know from Matthew 24:36 that no one except the Father will know the day or hour of the rapture.

Edgar C. Whisenant book *On Borrowed Time* seems to have been the first to equate the seven and a half days of silence in heaven of Revelation 8:1 to seven and a half days on earth.[3] Though he did not make the association with Luke 17:22–30 and the seven days of Genesis 7:4, 10 before the flood (wrath of God) to determine the duration of the seventh opened seal.

This analysis seems to point to the rapture occurring on one of two days, either the seventh day or the eighth day. Adding confidence to this two-day rapture window interpretation is that Revelation 8:1 does not say there was silence in heaven for *less than* half an hour. Instead Scripture says "there was silence in heaven for about half an hour." The word "about" in Scripture helps to support this two-day rapture window, placing the rapture event either just before or after the seven-and-a-half days of silence.

Adding additional strength to this interpretation is Kevin Howard and Marvin Rosenthal's book *The Feasts of the Lord*, which directly associates the rapture with the Feast of Trumpets. A second day of watchfulness by the rabbis is reflective of the two-day window for the rapture.

---

3   Edgar C. Whisenant, *On Borrowed Time*, © 1988, World Bible Society, 23.

It occurs at the New Moon when only the slightest crescent is visible. However, clouds could obscure the moon, and witnesses were required in ancient days. Watchfulness was a critical ingredient of this feast. The rabbis later added a second day to this feast to make sure they did not miss it. This need for watchfulness and preparedness in connection with the Feast of Trumpets is echoed and reechoed throughout the New Testament in connection with Messiah's coming.[4]

"Now when these things begin to take place, straighten up and raise your heads, because your redemption is drawing near" (Luke 21:28). Each row of figure 6 shows how a common theme of Scriptures supports the rapture in Revelation 8:5. Figure 7 shows the sequence of these chronological events. During the first great eschatological theophany of Revelation 8:5, the sun may temporally be blocked with a thick cloud (as it was during the great theophany at Mt. Sinai in Ex. 19:16), though the lightning flashes should provide some light. Since no one knows the hour of the rapture (Matt. 24:36), this thick cloud may last longer than an hour before the rapture.

DEFINITION OF SECULAR LIGHT AND DARKNESS

Luke 17:26–30 has planting and building when the rapture occurs, which indicates secular daylight versus priestly type of light definition for daily sacrifices.[5] In other parts of the world, it will be dark: "In that night there will be two in one bed. One will be taken and the other left" (Luke 17:34). Therefore, this author interprets these events as occurring during a normal, twenty-four-hour day of night and day, which will be labeled as "light." In contrast, the events of the sixth open seal, when the "sun became black as sackcloth" (Rev. 6:12b) will be labeled as "darkness," interpreted as a twenty-four-hour-a-day event.

---

4   Kevin Howard and Marvin Rosenthal, *The Feasts of the Lord: God's Prophetic Calendar from Calvary to the Kingdom* (Nashville: Thomas Nelson, 1997), 28.
5   See chapter 4, premise 4 for what a priest light definition is.

FIGURE 6: RAPTURE AND WRATH

Genesis	Luke and 2 Thess. 2	1 Timothy 4 and Matthew 24	Revelation 6, 7, and 8
	Sun, moon, and stars (darkness) (Luke 21:25)	Great tribulation ends (Matt. 24:29)	Opened seal 6: Sun like sackcloth (darkness) (6:12)
"For in seven days" (v. 7:4a)	Planting as in the days of Lot (light) (Luke 17:26–28)	Two men in a field (light) (Matt. 24:40)	Opened seal 7: Silence in heaven for about half an hour (7.5 days) (see figure 5; 8:1)
	Marriages again before wrath (Luke 17:17b)	Marriages forbidden earlier (1 Tim. 4:1–3)	
Rain for forty days and forty nights (wrath) (v. 7:4b)	Rapture and wrath on same day (Luke 17:27–30)	One man in a field taken, one left behind (Matt. 24:40)	144,000 and multitude in heaven (ch. 7) Rapture (8:5) followed by wrath (8:7ff.)
	Lightning flashes with Son of Man (Luke 17:24–26)		Lightning flashes in theophany (8:5)

FIGURE 7: SEVENTH OPENED SEAL TIMELINE

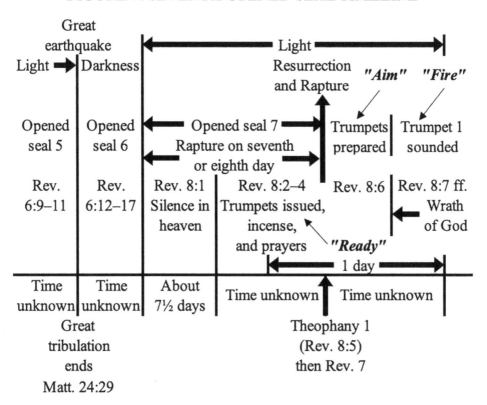

TIME DILATION IN HEAVEN

This theory is supported by Einstein's special theory of relativity, which describes how motion in space alters the flow of time, an effect known as time dilation. The effect is measured by the Lorentz transformation or factor. This time dilation increases as one approaches the speed of light. Steven Weinberg's *Foundations of Modern Physics*, quoted below, provides a known time dilation for the decay of unstable muon particles with a Lorentz factor (γ) of about ten times. The importance of this proven time dilation cannot be understated. An even faster speed, approaching the speed of light, would allow for Daniel's prophetic time ratio of 360:1.

At rest, muons, are observed to decay with a mean lifetime 2.2 microseconds, but although they are typically produced at an altitude of about 15 kilometers, a good fraction of these muons reach the ground before decaying, so even traveling near the speed of light they must have survived for a time (as measured on the earth's surface) at least 15 kilometers/300,000 kilometers/ second = 50 microseconds, and more if they reach the ground at a slant. ... Evidently the life of these muons is extended by their motion by a factor γ at least of order 10, which requires their velocity to be within a fraction of a percent of the speed of light.[6]

RESURRECTION THEN RAPTURE: DAY OF CHRIST

The first great eschatological theophany occurs in Revelation 8:5, which describes "peals of thunder, rumblings, flashes of lightning, and an earthquake." In Revelation 4:5, when the apostle John was in heaven, there was a theophany of "flashes of lightning, and rumblings and peals of thunder" coming from the throne. The difference being there was no earthquake in heaven. The one on the throne was identified as the Lord God Almighty from Revelation 4:8–10. So this seems to indicate that where Scripture speaks of "peals of thunder, rumblings, flashes of lightning, and an earthquake," it indicates the presence of the Lord and an earthly event. The well-known rapture event of Matthew 24:27 directly equates the lightning coming from the east to the coming (*parousia*) of the Son of Man, known as the rapture.

Adding strength to the idea of Revelation 8:5 describing the rapture of the elect is that the next two verses describe the wrath of God, starting with the trumpets being issued and then the first trumpet blown. As discussed earlier, the rapture and wrath of God must be on the same day. Having these three verses back-to-back provides significant evidence for the Beyond Prewrath position. If Revelation 8:5 is the rapture, then the multitude rejoicing in heaven in Revelation 7:9–17 must be the consequence of this event on earth. Also, the 144,000 being sealed in Revelation 7:1–8 would seem to occur chronologically after the rapture.

---

6   Steven Weinberg, *Foundations of Modern Physics*, University Printing House, Cambridge, CB2 8BS, United Kingdom, © 2021, 104.

Deuteronomy 33:2 also associates lightning with His coming in the Sinai theophany: "[H]e came from the ten thousands of holy ones, with flaming fire at his right hand."

> Then the angel took the censer and filled it with fire from the altar and threw it on the earth, and there were *peals of thunder, rumblings, flashes of lightning, and an earthquake.* (Rev. 8:5, emphasis added)

JEWISH TRIBES MISS THE FIRST RAPTURE

During this rapture theophany, "he is coming with the clouds, and every eye will see him, even those who pierced him, and all tribes of the earth will wail on account of him. Even so. Amen" (Rev. 1:7). The Jewish tribes, observing their Messiah in the clouds, will wail, which seems to be when their spiritual eyes begin to open slowly. As Paul says, "So I ask, did they stumble in order that they might fall? By no means! Rather, through their trespass salvation has come to the Gentiles, so as to make Israel jealous" (Rom. 11:11). Later in chapter 8 of this book, we will see that Revelation 11:19 describes a second rapture for the Jewish people who will earlier be saved as new believers in Christ.

Revelation 1:7 indicates that those with the mark of the beast are not the ones wailing that they missed the rapture. "God sends them a strong delusion, so that they may believe what is false, in order that all may be condemned who did not believe the truth but had pleasure in unrighteousness" (2 Thess. 2:11–12).

SECOND AND THIRD GREAT ESCHATOLOGICAL THEOPHANIES

The description of the theophany in Revelation 8:5 (first theophany), "peals of thunder, rumblings, flashes of lightning, and an earthquake" also occurs in Revelation 11:19 (second theophany) and 16:18 (third theophany), though 16:18 describes "a great earthquake." These last two theophanies appear to have eschatological implications beyond the resurrection and rapture of the elect (church) in Revelation 8:5, called the day of Christ. They seem to indicate that the Lord will give humanity a total of three eschatological opportunities to be saved.[7] Figure 8 represents the first, second, and third great eschatological theophanies occur during the seventh opened seal in Revelation 8:5, the seventh blown trumpet in Revelation 11:19, and the seventh poured bowl in Revelation 16:18.

FIGURE 8: THREE GREAT ESCHATOLOGICAL THEOPHANIES

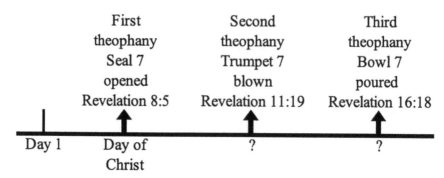

LIGHTNING: THE MEANS OF RAPTURE TO THE SKY

Associated with each of these three great theophanies is lightning. In Luke 17:24–26, we see lightning is directly associated with the eschatological return of the Son of Man. Job 36:32 says, "He covers His hands with the lightning, And commands it to strike the target" (NASB). Habakkuk 3:4 also associates lightning with his power: "His brightness was like the light; rays flashed from his hand; and there he veiled his power." Consider that Elijah is the only man who has ever been taken alive to heaven and was seen by someone (Elisha). Elijah's "chariots of fire and horses of fire" in 2 Kings 2:11 could be the same symbolism of lightning found in Revelation 8:5, 11:19, and 16:18, which is proposed as the means of being taken (raptured) to meet Jesus in the sky. See also Habakkuk 3:11, and Luke 17:24–26.

These scriptures indicate that each lightning flash may indicate how each Christian believer will be physically taken in the rapture. As ironic as it seems, believers might want to be struck by lightning to be physically raptured to meet Jesus in the sky (1 Thess. 4:17).

---

7   For more details on this exciting new eschatology understanding, see chapter 8.

SATAN THROWN FROM HEAVEN "LIKE LIGHTNING"

Some might ask "What about lightning being associated when Satan was thrown from heaven?" Luke 10:18 says, "He said to them, 'I saw Satan fall like lightning from heaven.'" When one considers that scripture says *like* lightning and not just lightning, we can see why this analogy is not applicable. Another analogy is Satan disguising himself as an angel of light (2 Cor. 11:14) in order to deceive us.

EACH THEOPHANY FOR A MULTITUDE

Some may say equating these three theophanies to a rapture is not reasonable since there are other scripture references (see chapter 1, note 3) that do not have this same theophany phrase, but consider that some of these other rapture scriptures are only for one or two people and not a multitude, which could be part of the reason for the difference.

THE GREAT THEOPHANY AT MT. SINAI

A well-known theophany is the great theophany at Mt. Sinai, where the marriage covenant between Israel and God was confirmed (Ex. 19:16–20). Exodus 19:16 describes thunder, lightning flashes, and a thick cloud associated with this theophany. Exodus 19:18–20 describes fire, smoke, a violent earthquake, sound of a trumpet growing louder and then thunder when God spoke. All of this indicates that the Lord himself was present in the cloud and fire. This is representative of the Lord's presence, though not of a rapture.

THE TRUMPETS PREPARED (AIM) AND THE FIRST BLOWN (FIRE)

The first blown trumpet is considered to be the start of the third eschatological wrath of God.[8] A military analogy to Revelation 8:6–7 is "aim" and "fire."

---

8   For the first and second eschatological wrath of God, see chapters 7 and 8.

Now the seven angels who had the seven trumpets *prepared to blow them* ["aim"]. *The first angel blew his trumpet* ["fire"], and there followed hail and fire, mixed with blood, and these were thrown upon the earth. And a third of the earth was burned up, and a third of the trees were burned up, and all green grass was burned up. (Rev. 8:6–7, emphasis added)

MAIN REASONS FOR A RAPTURE IN REVELATION 8:5

We can now summarize the main reasons for the proposed rapture of the elect occurring in Revelation 8:5:

First, the rapture and the wrath of God must occur on the same day as in the days of Noah and Lot (Luke 17:22–30). This same day event seems to be reflective of the back-to-back verses of Revelation 8:5 and 8:6–7ff.

Second, the same phrase describing the eschatological theophany of Revelation 8:5 can only be found in Revelation 11:19 and 16:18. These theophanies provide support for a second rapture event (spiritually saved Israel being raptured) who attend the béma judgment with the elect, and third the sheep and goats. The lightning within each theophany is directly associated with the presence of the Lord God Almighty in Revelation 4:5, 8–10, as with Israel and Moses in Mt. Sinai.

> He covers his hands with the *lightning* and commands it to strike the mark. (Job 36:32, emphasis added)

> The sun and moon stood still in their place at the *light of your arrows* as they sped, at the *flash of your glittering spear*. (Hab. 3:11, emphasis added)

> For as the *lightning flashes* and lights up the sky from one side to the other, so will the Son of Man be in his day (rapture). (Luke 17:24, emphasis added)

Third, many scholars consider the sixth opened seal of the wrath of the Lamb to be when the wrath of God begins with its earlier and same day rapture. They use Acts 2:17–21 and Joel 2:28–32 as support. But these verses describe an event involving darkness, blood, and fire. Nowhere do all three occur during the sixth opened seal. They only occur during the Jehoshaphat campaign of the sixth blown trumpet.[9]

Fourth, the multitude in heaven in Revelation 7:9–17 should chronologically follow the rapture in Revelation 8:5, though it precedes it sequentially in Scripture.

Fifth, during the seventh opened seal, those with the mark of the beast are marrying again according to Jesus's prophetic analogy to his eschatological return in Luke 17:27. We know the majority, if not all, of the marriages will be for those with the mark of the beast, who worship its image, since they are also planting and building. Believers should realize they would not be on earth long enough to enjoy the fruits of their labor by planting and building. Planting and building indicates light, which is not present during the sixth opened seal of Revelation 6:12–17. The rapture will occur on either the seventh or eighth day after entering the light of the seventh opened seal.

Sixth, during the tribulation of the fourth opened seal and great tribulation of the fifth opened seal, those who apostatize are forbidden to marry (1 Tim. 4:1–3). Returning to normal life with marriages when the seventh seal is opened is reflective of the seven days of Genesis 7:4, before the Noah flood came and swept the unrighteous away. The half hour of silence in heaven in Revelation 8:1 was converted to exactly seven and a half days on earth, which points to these seven days before the flood. Since no one knows the exact day of His return, the rapture seems to occur on either the seventh or eighth day after leaving the darkness of the sixth opened seal.

CONCLUSION

The following conclusions are provided for consideration:

The rapture occurs in Revelation 8:5, leading to the 144,000 sealed and the multitude in heaven in Revelation 7. The Revelation 8:5 theophany phrase of "peals of thunder, rumblings, flashes of lightning, and an earthquake" indicates the rapture. Within this phrase, *lightning* (Luke 17:24–26; Job 36:32, 2 Kings 2:11, Hab. 3:11) was shown as the means of being taken (raptured) from the earth to meet Jesus in the clouds. Revelation 8:1–5 occurs chronologically before Revelation 7. Revelation 8:5 followed by the wrath of God in Revelation 8:6–7 provides strong evidence for the Beyond Prewrath

---

9   For more details, see chapter 2.

position. Since not all Scripture is chronological, this non–chronological interpretation of John's prophetic events seems to have merit.

The unique second great eschatological theophany in Revelation 11:19 and the third great eschatological theophany in Revelation 16:18 have prophetic implications beyond the first great eschatology theophany of Revelation 8:5.

The rapture and wrath appear to be on the seventh or eighth day of the seventh opened seal. The start of the seventh opened seal will be recognized by leaving the darkness of the sixth opened seal and entering the light of the seventh opened seal. Since this theory does not specify a specific one–day of Jesus' return it is in agreement with Matthew 24:36 of not knowing the day or hour of his return.

The three great eschatological theophanies, as shown in figure 8, forms the number 777. The number seven is considered perfect and a day of rest.

Chapter 4

Daniel 8:13–14: 2,300 Evenings and Mornings

PURPOSE

In this chapter, we will analyze the 2,300 evenings and mornings of Daniel 8:13–14 to determine a range of days for the sixth opened seal. Second, a partial near and full far prophecy fulfillment Daniel 8:13–14 will be proposed with Antiochus IV and the future Antichrist, respectively.

> Then I heard a holy one speaking, and another holy one said to the one who spoke, "For how long is the vision concerning the regular burnt offering, the transgression that makes desolate, and the giving over of the sanctuary and host to be trampled underfoot?" And he said to me, "For 2,300 evenings and mornings. Then the sanctuary shall be restored to its rightful state." (Dan. 8:13–14)

SIX PREMISES

The following six premises form the basis for understanding this prophetic mystery:

1) The third temple (building) or tabernacle (tent-like structure) will first be built in Jerusalem with animal sacrifices. "And he shall make a strong covenant with many for one week, and for half of the week he shall put an end to sacrifice and offering" (Dan. 9:27a).

2) The holy one of Daniel 8:13 asks the question, and the other holy one of Daniel 8:14 answers the question. This then forms an equation of equality where the question equals the answer.

3) Daniel 12:12 extends the 1,290 days of events in Daniel 12:11 to 1,335 days.

4) The 2,300 evenings and mornings of Daniel 8:14 are 1,150 days. Then the sanctuary will be restored to its rightful state. One evening and one morning of sacrifice are defined as a day of light.

5) Days of darkness mixed with days of light must be included with the holy one's answer on the right side of the equation to count all the continuous days in premise 2.

6) The seven poured bowls are thirty days long from Day 1,261 to Day 1,290.

LITTLE HORN BACKGROUND

Daniel 8 records Daniel's second vision. In it he saw a ram, representing the kings of Media and Persia, and a goat, representing the king of Greece. The goat overpowered the ram, though it lost its large horn. In its place, four horns came up, and then among them another horn came up and grew in power (Dan. 8:1–9). We know from the interpretation of Daniel's first vision that the horns are kings in Daniel 7:24. This little horn who grew in power is the one who will desecrate the third temple and stop the daily sacrifices (Dan. 8:9–12). However, this author will provide evidence that he will give away his kingdom and then become the man of lawlessness spoken about in 2 Thessalonians 2.[1]

2,300 EVENINGS AND MORNINGS

The priests in the temple offered two regular burnt offerings every day: the first in the evening at sunset and the next in the morning (Ex. 29:38–39). The idea that Daniel 8:13–14 equates to 2,300 days does not seem eschatological reasonable for four reasons, which provides support for premise 4:

1) 2,300 days would equate to over six years. Since the holy one in Daniel 8:13 says this begins at the desolation of the sanctuary (considered to be Day 1 in Dan. 9:27 and Rev. 11:1), then 2,300 days later would place the end almost three years into the millennium. Trying to interpret the vision past Day 1,335 (Dan. 12:12) makes no eschatological sense. Only using 1,150 days (part of the right side of the equation) would make sense as shown later in equation 2ff.

---

1   See chapter 5.

2) Antiochus's desecration of the first temple was, in many ways, a prophetic partial near view of the Antichrist's desecration of the future third temple.[2]

3) Although most Bible versions have 2,300 evenings and mornings, the New King James Version has 2,300 days, and *The Cambridge Bible for Schools and Colleges* has 1,150 days. So there is not complete unity in the church as to how many days are in Daniel 8:14.

> *unto two thousand and three hundred* **evenings, mornings**] i.e. successive evenings and mornings: cf. Daniel 8:26 'the vision of the evenings and the mornings.' The expression is peculiar; but it seems to have been suggested by the fact that the burnt-offering (Daniel 8:11; Daniel 8:13) was offered morning and evening daily (Exodus 29:38–42); the meaning consequently is that this offering would cease for 2300 times, i.e. during 1150 days.[3]

4) The Expanded Bible has both 1,150 and 2,300 days as a possible interpretation.

> The angel said to me, "This will happen for twenty–three hundred evenings and mornings [*either 2,300 or 1,150 days*]. Then the holy place [sanctuary] will be repaired [restored; made right again]. (Dan. 8:14 EXB, emphasis added)

NEAR-FAR PROPHECY

The first celebration of Hanukkah as a consequence of the actions of Antiochus Epiphanes provide an example of the near part of a near-far prophecy. Antiochus desecrated the second temple in 168 BC. Several years later, Judas Maccabeus, with his brothers and fellow Hebrews, was able to recapture Jerusalem after a series of battles. They reconstructed a second

---

2 Kevin Howard and Marvin Rosenthal, *The Feasts of the Lord: God's Prophetic Calendar from Calvary to the Kingdom* (Nashville: Thomas Nelson, 1997), 173.

3 Herbert Edward Ryle, *The Cambridge Bible for Schools and Colleges* (Cambridge: Cambridge University Press, 1881), Daniel 8:14, Bible Hub, https://biblehub.com/commentaries/cambridge/daniel/8.htm.

temple on the 25th of Kislev in 165 BC.[4] Since then, the Jews celebrate the 25th of Kislev, called Hanukkah or the Feast of Dedication. as a memorial to the purification and rededication of the temple in Jerusalem. Hanukkah is not one of feasts of the Lord in the Old Testament, since the events it celebrates occurred during the time between the Old and New Testaments.[5] Jesus celebrated the Feast of Dedication in John 10:22.

This indicates that the prophecy in Daniel 8:11–14 is a near-far prophecy. Parts of Daniel 8 were fulfilled with the desolation of the second temple in 168 BC, though its far eschatological fulfillment for the third temple has yet to happen. Why was the prophecy not fully fulfilled in 168 BC? First, the time from when Antiochus Epiphanes, the king of Syria, ended the temple sacrifices to when they restarted was exactly three years.[6] This was not the required three and a half years in the second half of the seventieth week of Daniel. Second, in 165 BC, the Daniel timeline had about another 200 years before the sixty-nine prophetic years (483 Daniel years) were completed. Third, and most importantly, no rapture-type event occurred during these years.

DAY 1,260: ISRAEL RAPTURE EVENT?

Before regular burnt offerings can begin for the fourth temple in the millennium, it must be dedicated on Hanukkah. In their book *The Feasts of the Lord*, Kevin Howard and Marvin Rosenthal place this holiday beginning seventy-five days after Yom Kippur, Israel's Day of Atonement.[7] In chapter 3 we noted that the rapture of the church in Revelation 8:5 uses the same theophany language as Revelation 11:19, which occurs at the end of the seventh blown trumpet, the last of the seven blown trumpets, which ends the seventieth week of Daniel. Also, when the dragon (Satan) is thrown down to earth in Revelation 12:13, he then pursues the woman (Israel), who is provided for 1,260 days in Revelation 12:6. The first theophany occurs in one day. These different forms of analysis indicate that Israel may have a rapture on Day 1,260. Therefore, it is likely that regular burnt offerings will

4   Sam Nadler, *Messiah in The Feasts of Israel* (Charlotte, NC: Word of Messiah Ministries, 2006), 178.
5   Ibid., 180.
6   Ibid., 178.
7   Howard and Rosenthal, *Feasts of the Lord*, 159.

begin seventy-five days later, which is Day 1,335. Day 1,335 expected to represent the start of the millennium.

HOW LONG IS THE VISION (LEFT SIDE OF THE EQUATION)?

The holy one in Daniel 8:13 asked a question composed of three parts: "For how long is the vision concerning [1] the regular burnt offering, [2] the transgression that makes desolate, and [3] the giving over of the sanctuary and host to be trampled underfoot?" The book of Daniel later answers the first two questions: "And from the time that the regular burnt offering is taken away and the abomination that makes desolate is set up, there shall be 1,290 days. Blessed is he who waits and arrives at the 1,335 days" (Dan. 12:11–12). Revelation provides the third answer: "But do not measure the court outside the temple; leave that out, for it is given over to the nations, and they will trample the holy city for forty-two months [1,260 days]" (Rev. 11:2).

So the answer to the first two questions is 1,335 days. The answer to third question is forty-two months (1,260 days). Therefore, 1,335 days is the longest duration for the left side of the equation in premise 3.

DARKNESS (PART OF RIGHT SIDE OF THE EQUATION)

Over these 1,335 days, we need to determine how many days of darkness there are. There are six Scriptural events of darkness to be examined during these days from Day 1 to Day 1,335.

1) Fifth opened seal, Day 1: "And there shall be a unique day, which is known to the LORD, neither day nor night, but at evening time there shall be light" (Zech. 14:7). This day is the day of the Lord, called the Jerusalem campaign (Zech. 14:1–2). Sacrifices could have occurred in the evening with the light, though not in the morning with darkness. Therefore, a half a day of darkness will be assigned for the morning.

2) Sixth opened seal: The duration is unknown (Rev. 6:12–17).

3) Fourth blown trumpet: "A third of the sun was struck" (Rev. 8:12a), so there was enough sun for the priests to offer sacrifices. "And a third of the moon, and a third of the stars, so that a third of their light

might be darkened" (Rev. 8:12b) is during the night, so it does not affect the sacrifices during the day. The Scripture concern relative to the twice daily sacrifices is "and a third of the day might be kept from shining" (Rev. 8:12c). This author will assume "a third of the day" to be a block of darkness duration. For example, if there are twelve hours of normal light, then four hours would be darkness. If darkness happened in the morning at sunrise, from say 6 am to 10 am, then the priest would have had their morning sacrifice at 10 am instead of 6 am, therefore not affecting their twice-a-day sacrifice. This logic seems to hold regardless of when the block of darkness would happen during the day. This author considers the fourth blown trumpet of limited darkness to not have an impact on the priestly sacrifices, and therefore no variable for darkness will be assigned.

4) Fifth blown trumpet: The duration is five months or 150 days (Rev. 9:1–11).

5) Sixth blown trumpet: The duration is two days (Joel 2:31; Rev. 14:17–19).[8]

6) Fifth poured bowl: Duration is unknown (Dan. 12:11; Rev. 12:6; 15; 16:10).

The equation for darkness now becomes:

Darkness = fifth opened seal (S5) + sixth opened seal (S6) + fifth blown trumpet (T5) + sixth blown trumpet (T6) + fifth poured bowl (B5)

Equation 1: Darkness = S5 (0.5 day) + S6 + T5 (150 days) + T6 (2 days) + B5 (between 1 and 30 days)

FORMING THE BASIC EQUATION AND DETERMINING THE LENGTH OF DARKNESS

The holy one's question in Daniel 8:13 will form the left side of the equation per premise 2. This was previously equated to 1,335 days. The holy one's answer in Daniel 8:14 will form the equivalent right side of the equation. This right side of the equation must be composed of the number of days of light needed for determining when a burnt offering could be made (sunset and

---

8   See chapter 8.

morning) and the number of days of darkness, when no sunset or morning would be available for a burnt offering.

This is not a question of whether the priests will have artificial lighting available to perform the burnt offerings, since we know they had oil lamps for lighting in the Bible. The parable of the ten virgins in Matthew 25:1–13 referenced oil lamps for lighting. This is a question of recognizing the location of the sun in the sky to determine sunset and morning. Although, darkness was not specifically mentioned in Daniel 8:14, we know that between Day 1 and Day 1,335 there are several events of darkness, which must be included for equality to the left side of the equation.

Question in Daniel 8:13 = Answer in Daniel 8:14

Equation 2: length of the vision = days of light + days of darkness

1,335 days = 1,150 days + days of darkness

Darkness = 185 days

SOLVING FOR THE DURATION OF THE SIXTH OPENED SEAL

There are two unknowns in equation 1. The duration of the fifth poured bowl is tightly bound by thirty days with a total of seven poured bowls. The sixth opened seal is the least bound since it is during the second half of Daniel's seventieth week of three-and-a-half years. Knowing the duration of the sixth opened seal is the most valuable for believers since it is after the great tribulation but before the first eschatological day of Christ (rapture). So to solve for S6, we will insert the previously determined length of darkness, 185 days, into equation 1.

185 days = S5 (0.5 day) + S6 + T5 (150 days) + T6 (2 days) + B5 (between 1 and 30 days)

S6 = 185 days – [(0.5 + 150 + 2) days + B5 (between 1 and 30 days)]

S6 = 185 days – 152.5 days – B5 (between 1 and 30 days)

Equation 3: S6 = 32.5 days – B5 (between 1 and 30 days)

S6 (minimum) = 32.5 – 30 = 2.5 days

S6 (maximum) = 32.5 – 1 = 31.5 days

S6 (sixth opened seal) = 2.5 to 31.5 days

TIGHTENING THE RANGE OF SIXTH OPENED SEAL

The range for the duration of the sixth opened seal can be tightened significantly by using an approximation. The average duration of the seven poured bowls over the thirty days would be slightly over four days for each poured bowl. The description of people gnawing their tongues in anguish and cursing the God of heaven for their pain and sores during the fifth poured bowl of darkness seems to suggest an average duration, if not less, when compared to the descriptions of the other six poured bowls (Rev. 16:10–11). The sixth poured bowl description of the kings traveling from east of the Euphrates seems to suggest the longest event (Rev. 16:12). This limited analysis should allow the estimated duration of the fifth poured bowl to be bound more tightly than thirty days. This author therefore considers a maximum of a five-day duration for the fifth poured bowl to be reasonable.[9]

---

9   If the duration of the fifth poured bowl seems too tight or too loosely bound, the given equations can be used to calculate an alternative.

Equation 3: $S6 = 32.5$ days $- B5$ (between 1 and 30 days)

$S6 \approx 32.5$ days $- B5$ (about 1 to 5 days)

$S6$ (minimum) $\approx 32.5 - 5$ days $= 27.5$ days

$S6$ (maximum) $\approx 32.5 - 1$ day $= 31.5$ days

$S6 \approx 27.5$ to 31.5 days

If this is correct, it would significantly tighten the possible duration of the sixth opened seal. To simplify these fractions of a day for figure 9, the range will be loosened to a six-day range of whole numbers between twenty-seven and thirty-two days.

PROOF FOR PREMISE 3

To show that the length of the vision in Daniel 8:13 begins at Day 1,335, rather than on Day 1,290, we will determine the minimum number of days possible for the right side of equation 1 for Daniel 8:14. We will then compare that with the left side of the equation for Daniel 8:13. If the result is more than 1,290 days, it would then confirm premise 3.

Equation 1: darkness $= S5$ (0.5 day) $+ S6 + T5$ (150 days) $+ T6$ (2 days) $+ B5$ (between 1 and 30 days)

Equation 2: (length of the vision) $=$ (days of light $+$ days of darkness)

We will solve for the length of the vision by inserting equation 1 for darkness into equation 2.

length of the vision $=$ [(days of light) $+ S5$ (0.5 day) $+ S6 + T5$ (150 days) $+ T6$ (2 days) $+ B5$ (between 1 and 30 days)]

To determine the minimum number of days for the length of the vision, we will minimize the variables on the right side of the equation. The variable B5, which has a range between one and thirty days, will be set to the minimum of one day. S6 will be also be set to the minimum of one day. The 1,150 days known for duration for light and T5 of two days will also be inserted.

Minimum length of the vision = 1,150 days + 0.5 day + 1 day+ 150 days
+ 2 days + 1 day

Minimum length of the vision = 1,304.5 days

This analysis shows the length of at least one of the three visions in Daniel 8:13 must be at least 1,304.5 days. Since 1,304.5 days is more than the 1,290 days of Daniel 12:11 but less than or equal to the 1,335 days of Daniel 12:12, this adds confidence that we should apply the 1,335 days as the length of the vision (left side of the equation).

PROOF FOR PREMISE 4

Equation 2 showed that the length of the vision (1,335 days of Daniel 12:11–12) equaled the number of days of light and days of darkness. Daniel 8:14 is sometimes interpreted as 2,300 days of light for temple sacrifices, though this does not make sense. Trying to use 2,300 days of interpreted light added to the days of darkness (also a positive number) can never equal the left side of the equation of 1,335 days. Only using the 1,150 days of light interpretation does the equation make sense.

1,335 days $\neq$ 2,300 days + days of darkness

CONCLUSION

The duration of the sixth opened seal appears to be between two and a half and thirty-one and a half days. There are six other poured bowls during the third septet, which allows the sixth opened seal duration to be tightened approximately to a range of twenty-seven to thirty-two days, which is a six-day window of duration.

FIGURE 9: TIMELINES FOR SIXTH AND SEVENTH OPENED SEALS

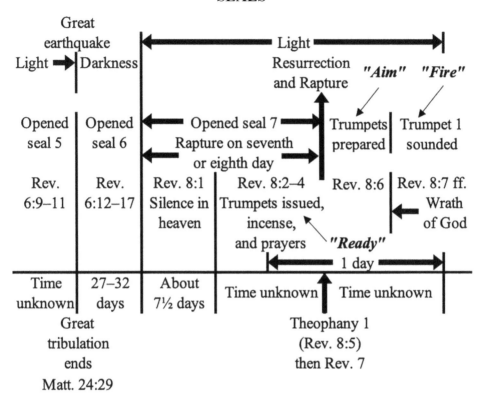

Chapter 5

Daniel Parallels and Goat-Ram Timeline

PURPOSE

This chapter presents three new possible eschatological understandings of Daniel:

1) There are parallels between the well-known first opened seal of Revelation 6:1–2 and the unknown equivalent of Daniel 7:8, 20, 24; 8:9, 23.

2) There are parallels on Day 1 between Matthew 24:15–21 and Daniel 7:11a, 20; 8:10–14, 24, 26.

3) Daniel 8:5–7 shows that the goat (Grecian kingdom) who counterattacks the ram (Media and Persia) may identify the specific country the man of lawlessness will come from. This counterattack will occur prior to the first opened seal.

PARALLELS BETWEEN DANIEL 2, 7, 8, 10, REVELATION 6, AND MATTHEW 24

The first four kingdoms of King Nebuchadnezzar's dream in Daniel 2 form a long chronology of about 2,600 years, where we are waiting for the revised fourth kingdom to start with the seventieth week of Daniel. Three eschatological military events, not related to Jesus's three later campaigns, may occur prior to the start of the second opened seal. The first two military events could be a prophetic near-far interpretation of Daniel's ram and goat. The first is the ram attacking in Daniel 8:3–4. The second is the goat counterattacking the ram in Daniel 8:5–7 and 10:20. The third military event in Daniel 7:8, 20, 24; 8:9, 23; and Revelation 6:1–2 is considered a peaceful conquest. This peaceful conquest occurs during the first opened seal when the little horn seems to be transitioning by giving up his kingdom to the man of lawlessness. These eschatological warfare events appear to occur during different chronological times. Daniel 8:3–8 is chronologically before Daniel 8:9, which provides some support for the battle between the goat and ram occurring before the peaceful conquest. Daniel 2:40–43; 7:7,

23–25; and 8:20–21 did not seem to be associated with the (a) ram attacks, (b) goat counterattacks, (c) four goat horns, (d) first opened seal or (e) Day 1. A cross-referenced chronology of common Scripture is shown in figure 10.

Some other cross references not included in the figure are (1) Daniel 7:12a ("their dominion was taken away") and Revelation 17:13 ("hand over their power and authority to the beast"), and (2) Daniel 7:11b ("the beast was killed, and its body destroyed and given over to be burned with fire") and Revelation 19:20 ("thrown alive into the lake of fire").

TEN KINGS OF THE REVIVED FOURTH KINGDOM

A distinction can be made to separate the fourth kingdom into two kingdoms: a historic fourth kingdom and an eschatological revived fourth kingdom with ten horns (kingdoms). This revived fourth kingdom can be supported since there is no reference to ten historical kings of warfare around Israel and associated with the Revelation 17 prophetic heads. Also supporting this revived fourth kingdom is the mortal wound that was healed in Revelation 13:12b.[1]

---

1   See chapter 9.

FIGURE 10: PARALLELS BETWEEN DANIEL 2, 7, 8, 10, MATTHEW 24, AND REVELATION 6

Daniel 2	Daniel 7 Vision 1	Daniel 8 Vision 2	Daniel 10 Vision 4	Kingdoms	Matt./ Rev.
vv. 37–38	vv. 4, 17			First kingdom: Babylonian lion	
v. 39	vv. 5, 17			Second kingdom: Medo-Persian bear	
v. 39	vv. 6, 17			Third kingdom: Grecian leopard	
v. 40	vv. 7, 17, 19			Fourth kingdom	
vv. 40–43	vv. 7, 23–25	vv. 20–21		Revived fourth kingdom	
		vv. 3–4		a. Ram attacks	
		vv. 5–7	v. 20	b. Goat counter-attacks	
		vv. 8, 22		c. Four goat horns	
	vv. 8, 20, 24	vv. 9, 23		d. First opened seal	Rev. 6:1, 2
	vv. 11a, 20	vv. 10–14, 24, 26		e. Day 1	Matt. 24:15–21
vv. 44–45	vv. 18, 21, 22, 26, 27	v. 25b		Fifth kingdom: Messianic	

NEAR–FAR PROPHECY

Daniel 8:1–8 could be a near-far prophecy. The near prophecy was fulfilled beginning with the death of Alexander the Great in 323 BC. His four generals eventually divided up his kingdom. The death of Alexander the Great fulfilled the large broken horn in Daniel 8:22. The four generals who divided up his kingdom are the four horns. The far prophecy has eschatological implications. The chronology points to the two warfare events of this far prophecy being fulfilled just prior to the start of the seventieth week of Daniel.

DANIEL 2 AND 7 (BIG PICTURE)

Daniel 2 and 7 provide a big picture of the rulers of King Nebuchadnezzar's prophetic kingdoms. Daniel 7 goes deeper into the eight rulers in verses 7, 8, 20, and 23–25. These deeper Daniel 7 verses are discussed next since they are associated with many of the verses in Daniel 8.

DANIEL 8 (SMALL PICTURE): WAR AND PEACEFUL CONQUEST

In Revelation 17:12 the apostle John identifies the ten horns as ten kings. "And the ten horns that you saw, they [ten kings] and the beast [man of lawlessness] will hate the prostitute" (Rev. 17:16a).

In Daniel 8:1–8 the ram attacks the goat and then the goat counterattacks, shattering his two horns. These should be considered destructive warfare events. The interpretation in Daniel 8:20–21 explains that the two-horned ram represents the kings of Media and Persia and the goat represents the king of Greece. The goat of the Grecian Empire would include not only present-day Greece but also countries along the eastern Mediterranean and extending inland into parts of Asia. This was the empire of Alexander the Great.

"Then the goat became exceedingly great" (Dan. 8:8a). The goat growing in power indicates that there was some amount of time from when the goat became the victor to when it lost its large horn. This is a prophetic representation of Alexander the Great dying while in power. "But when he was strong, the great horn was broken, and instead of it there came up four conspicuous horns toward the four winds of heaven" (Dan. 8:8b). These four horns of Daniel 8:8, 22 are important since they represent the approaching start of the seventieth week of Daniel, as shown in figures 10 and 11. "Out of one of them came a little horn, which grew exceedingly great toward the south, toward the east, and toward the glorious land" (Dan. 8:9).

Chronologically later and militarily distinct from these warfare events is Daniel 7:8 ("plucked up by the roots") and Daniel 7:24 ("put down"), which is more representative of what this author considers a peaceful conquest. This peaceful conquest appears to be the same as the first opened seal in Revelation 6:1–2 with the rider on the white horse having a bow, though no arrows or quiver. Both of these scriptural events seem to be describing the same event of a military show of force.

FIGURE 11 DISCUSSION

Figure 11 shows the timeline of the beast of the sea. The beast of the sea (Rev. 13:1) had ten horns existing prior to the warfare events. "It was different from all the beasts that were before it, and it had ten horns" (Dan. 7:7b). An assumption is made that the ram is not part of the ten horns. This is loosely based on the ram not attacking one of its own.

The first row of figure 11 shows the chronology of the nine horns. The nine horns do not seem to be mentioned in the battles until Day 1. So it seems reasonable to assume their numbers do not change during this chronology presented by Scripture. The second row represents the tenth horn, identified as the goat, which starts as one goat horn and also ends on Day 1 as one goat horn. This author believes the little horn will give up his kingdom (horn) to honor someone. "Those who acknowledge him he shall load with honor. He shall make them rulers over many and shall divide the land for a price" (Dan. 11:39b). Otherwise, on Day 1 the nine horns, and not the prophetic ten, would represent the beast of the sea. "And the ten horns that you saw are ten kings who have not yet received royal power, but they are to receive authority as kings for one hour, together with the beast" (Rev. 17:12). This interpretation of the little horn giving up his kingdom fits well into the chronologically later 2 Thessalonians 2 man of lawlessness, also called the son of destruction. The first two events in the third row represent the ram, identified as Media and Persia. The end of the third and fourth rows show when the spirit of Satan enters the man of lawlessness and they become the Antichrist.

The figure with the dashed boundary box around "1 Goat horn*" represents the man of lawlessness in Daniel 7:8 plucking the other three goat kings up by their roots. The two dashed boxes represent that the revealing of the man of lawlessness will not likely occur until Day 1.[2] See details in chapter 7. The beast of the sea will have ten horns and seven heads with ten diadems on its horns (Rev. 13:1).

FIGURE 11: TIMELINE OF THE BEAST OF THE SEA

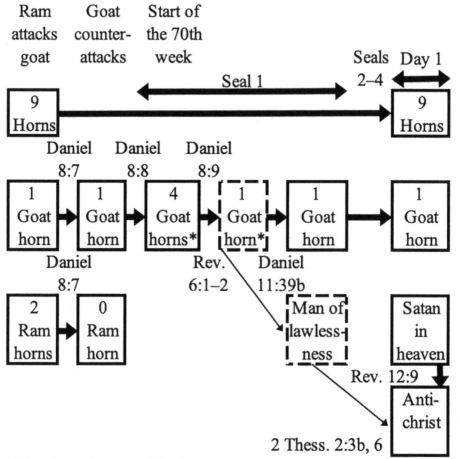

* Little horn is one of the horns

Dashed boxes: Likely known to only a few

---

2   See chapter 7.

OBSERVATIONS

Three observations can now be made.

First, there is an ongoing discussion among scholars concerning which country the man of lawlessness will come from. If Daniel 8:7–8 is a near-far prophecy, then it seems the country will be within the historic Grecian empire, which counterattacks the historic Medo-Persian empire. This counterattack would be expected to occur before the start of the seventieth week of Daniel.

Second, this analysis narrows down the list of the possible identities for man of lawlessness to only the four horns (kings) at the start of the seventieth week of Daniel. If any of these kings do not sign the covenant with Israel, then they would also be excluded as the possible man of lawlessness since he must make the covenant strong. "And he shall make a strong covenant with many for one week" (Dan. 9:27a). However, making it strong could also mean something else, such as providing financial support or a UN peace keeping force.

Third, the little horn is expected to give up his goat kingdom when the first seal is opened. This is in order to fulfill two scriptural prophecies. In Revelation 17:16, on Day 1 there are ten kings and one Antichrist. If he did not give up the goat kingdom, then there would be nine kings and not the ten prophetically required. This is since he cannot be both the Antichrist and one of his ten kings.[3] Also, when the little horn gives up the goat horn (Grecian kingdom), he will become the man of lawlessness. "Those who acknowledge him he shall load with honor. He shall make them rulers over many and shall divide the land for a price" (Dan. 11:39b).

IDENTIFYING THE BEAST WITH 666

It may be possible to identify and therefore reveal (2 Thess. 2:3) the man of lawlessness among the "many" of Daniel 9:27 which is before the abomination of desolation on Day 1. This is accomplished with interpreting Revelation 13:18. "This calls for wisdom: let the one who has understanding calculate the number of the beast [man of lawlessness], for it is the number of a man of lawlessness, and his number is 666." The challenge is what is the correct method of interpretation.

---

3   See chapter 9.

CONCLUSION

Parallels between Daniel and Revelation 6 provide clues about events that appear to occur prior to the start of the seventieth week of Daniel. This will provide astute believers advance warning of the start of the seventieth week.

Chapter 6

Parallels between Matthew 24 and Revelation 6–8

PURPOSE

In this chapter, we will present a case to show that the fourth opened seal is part of the first half of the seventieth week of Daniel and is associated with death and tribulation. This is partly based on the fourth opened seal likely being when the falling away occurs (2 Thess. 2:3–4) and the revealing of the man of lawlessness likely occurring on Day 1. The start of the 1,260 days of persecution with Satan being thrown from heaven in the second half of the seventieth help to support this position (Dan. 9:27; Rev. 12:6, 14; Rev. 13:5). Also, there is no tribulation when the sixth and seventh seals are opened.

PARALLELS WITH MATTHEW AND REVELATION

Figure 12 shows parallels between Matthew 24 and Revelation 6–8. As discussed later in this chapter, there is no tribulation when the sixth or seventh seals are opened. The wrath of God, associated with the same day rapture of the elect, does not begin until Revelation 8:7ff.

FIGURE 12: PARALLELS BETWEEN MATTHEW 24 AND REVELATION 6–8

Matthew 24	Parallels	Revelation 6, 8
vv. 4–5	Peaceful conquest (birth pangs)	Opened seal 1 (6:1–2)
vv. 6–7	Wars (birth pangs)	Opened seal 2 (6:3–4)
v. 7	Famines and earthquakes (birth pangs)	Opened seal 3 (6:5–6)
vv. 9–14	Death and tribulation (hard labor)	Opened seal 4 (6:7–8)
vv. 15–26	Martyrdom and great tribulation (hard labor)	Opened seal 5 (6:9–11)
v. 29	Wrath of the Lamb (no tribulation)	Opened seal 6 (6:12–17)
vv. 30–31, 37–42	Normal life, then rapture (no tribulation)	Opened seal 7 ("ready") (8:1–5)
vv. 37–42	Trumpets prepared and first trumpet blown till poured bowls are emptied (wrath of God)	Blown trumpet 1 ("aim" and "fire") (8:6ff.)

FIRST OPENED SEAL: PEACEFUL CONQUEST

Revelation 6:1–2 identifies the first opened seal with a rider on a prophetic white horse. The first opened seal parallels Matthew 24:4–5, where Jesus warns us that many will come in his name to deceive many. One way to describe this first opened seal is with the oxymoron phrase "a peaceful conquest." The rider in Revelation 6:2 has a bow, but there is no mention of arrows or a quiver. Having a bow means the rider is armed for war, as in 1 Chronicles 12:1–2. This military show of force also represents coming in false peace, as Jesus warned in Matthew 24:4–5.

Christ also rides a white horse in Revelation 19:11, but He does not arrive from heaven until later, during the thirty days of the poured bowls. In Revelation 19:15, Christ has a sharp sword—probably prophetic. So the rider from the first opened seal does not appear to be Jesus. Comparing Daniel 7:8, 24b; and Revelation 6:1–2 reveals that their descriptions of this peaceful conquest match closely. Therefore, the rider on the white horse from the first opened seal appears to be the little horn, who conquers under the guise of bringing peace.[1]

Daniel 7:24b parallels Revelation 6:1–2 in predicting that the little horn will "put down three kings." Some Bible versions use "subdue" or "lay low." This little horn is one of the kings of the Grecian Empire. Daniel 7:8b appears to reference the same event when it predicts that the little horn will pluck out three horns. Some Bible translations say "uprooted" or "torn away." Each horn represents a king, as in Daniel 7:24. These actions by the little horn seem to be more of a surgical removal of these leaders, which is again synonymous with the rider having no arrows in Revelation 6:1–2.

The start of the seventieth week of Daniel will be initiated by the covenant of death predicted in Isaiah 28:15. "And he [little horn] shall make a strong covenant with many for one [prophetic] week" (Dan. 9:27a). What does the Lord say about Israel signing covenants with other people? Israel was told, "You shall make no covenant with them and their gods. They shall not dwell in your land, lest they make you sin against me; for if you serve their gods, it will surely be a snare to you" (Ex. 23:32–33). Figure 13 provides this timeline of events.

FIGURE 13: TIMELINE OF START OF THE SEVENTIETH WEEK OF DANIEL

Isaiah 28	Daniel 7	Daniel 9	Revelation 4, 5, 6
	The seat was taken by the Ancient of Days (v. 9)		God seated on the throne (4:2, 11)
Covenant of death signed (v. 15)		The little horn makes strong a covenant (v. 27a)	Lion of the tribe of Judah opens the scroll and seven seals (5:5)
	Little horn uproots three horns (v. 8) Three kings put down (v. 24b)		First opened seal (rider with a bow but no arrows or quiver) (6:1–2)

---

1   See chapter 5.

I considered the horns, and behold, there came up among them another horn, a little one, before which three of the first horns were plucked up by the roots. And behold, in this horn were eyes like the eyes of a man, and a mouth speaking great things. (Dan. 7:8)

As for the ten horns, out of this kingdom ten kings shall arise, and another shall arise after them; he shall be different from the former ones, and shall put down three kings. (Dan. 7:24)

And Jesus answered them, "See that no one leads you astray. For many will come in my name, saying, 'I am the Christ,' and they will lead many astray." (Matt. 24:4–5)

Now I watched when the Lamb opened one of the seven seals, and I heard one of the four living creatures say with a voice like thunder, "Come!" And I looked, and behold, a white horse! And its rider had a bow, and a crown was given to him, and he came out conquering, and to conquer. (Rev. 6:1–2)

SECOND OPENED SEAL: WARS

Revelation 6:3–4 identifies the second opened seal with a second prophetic horse, a bright red one. Its rider has a great sword to end peace and make people kill each other. The second opened seal parallels Matthew 24:6–7, which predicts kingdoms waging war against kingdoms. In Revelation 6:8, when the fourth seal is opened, the total borders of allowed death are expanded to reach a quarter of the world's population. Therefore, it seems likely the man of lawlessness and ten kings are expanding their borders during this second opened seal.

And you will hear of wars and rumors of wars. See that you are not alarmed, for this must take place, but the end is not yet. For nation will rise against nation, and kingdom against kingdom. (Matt. 24:6–7a)

When he opened the second seal, I heard the second living creature say, "Come!" And out came another horse, bright red. Its rider was permitted to take peace from the earth, so that people should slay one another, and he was given a great sword. (Rev. 6:3–4)

THIRD OPENED SEAL: FAMINES AND EARTHQUAKES

Revelation 6:5–6 identifies the third opened seal with a third prophetic horse, a black one. "Its rider had a pair of scales in his hand" (Rev. 6:5b). Revelation 6:6 has wheat, barley, oil, and wine for sale. A pair of scales in the rider's hand seems to indicate that the rider will have control over much of the world's petroleum and grain supply. Petroleum is still the lifeblood of the world's commerce. The unique aspect about grain versus other food items is that it has a long shelf life. When Joseph implemented the interpretation of Pharaoh's dream during the seven years of plenty, he stored enough grain for the following seven years of famine. The third opened seal parallels the prophecy about "famines and earthquakes in various places" in Matthew 24:7b.

SEVEN END–TIME EARTHQUAKES

There are seven eschatological earthquakes, which form a septet. Four are great earthquakes and three described as just an earthquake (labeled as regular). They are in the sequence of regular (Rev. 6:5–6 and Matt. 24:7), great (Zech. 14:4–10 and Ezek. 38:19), great (Rev. 6:12), regular (Rev. 8:5), great (Rev. 11:13), regular (11:19), and great (16:18).

The fifth (great) earthquake is at the end of the sixth blown trumpet and the sixth (regular) earthquake is in the seventh blown trumpet. The sixth earthquake following the fifth so quickly should be considered an aftershock.

The elect will live to feel the first four earthquakes up to when they are raptured, Although since the second earthquake on Day 1 has the epicenter in Israel, many through out the world may not feel it. When the bride of Christ likely returns to participate in the Armageddon battle they should feel the sixth earthquake.

The seventh and last quake in Revelation 16:18 (end of third septet) is "such as there had never been since man was on the earth, so great was that earthquake," so severe that it does not appear to have an aftershock.

FIGURE 14: SEVEN EARTHQUAKES

Type of Earthquake	Scripture	When
First: Various earthquakes	Rev. 6:5–6 and Matt. 24:7	Third opened seal
Second: Great earthquake (main)	Zech. 14:4–5, 10 and Ezek. 38:19	Fifth opened seal (Day 1)
Third: Great earthquake (main)	Rev. 6:12	Sixth opened seal
Fourth: Earthquake (aftershock)	Rev. 8:5	End of seventh opened seal
Fifth: Great earthquake (main)	Rev. 11:13	End of sixth blown trumpet (Day 1,259?)
Sixth: Earthquake (aftershock)	Rev. 11:19	End of seventh blown trumpet (Day 1,260)
Seventh: Great earthquake (main)	Rev. 16:18	End of seventh poured bowl (Day 1,290)

FOURTH OPENED SEAL: DEATH AND TRIBULATION

Matthew 24:9 identifies the fourth opened seal with tribulation and death. Since Satan does not arrive on earth until Day 1 this cannot be called Satan's great tribulation. It could appropriately be called the man of lawlessness tribulation. The fourth opened seal parallels Matthew 24:9–14. Revelation 6:7–8 identifies it with a fourth prophetic horse, a pale one whose rider causes death. A pale horse seems to represent the colorless appearance of the skin to symbolize death. Revelation 6:8a identifies the rider's name as Death, and Hades followed behind. Death represents a physical first death on earth, and Hades represents an eternal damnation of suffering in hell. Hades following Death seems to be analogous to the rebellion of Christians from their faith, described in 2 Thessalonians 2:1–3, occurring before the first eschatological day of the Lord.

FOURTH OPENED SEAL: STARTS BEFORE DAY 1

One of the insights that helps understand the chronology of the fourth opened seal in relation to Day 1 is in 2 Thessalonians 2:3a: "Let no one deceive you in any way. For that day will not come, unless the rebellion comes first." "That day" is what this author considers the first eschatological day of the Lord. Chapter 7 provides support for the idea that the first eschatological day of the Lord is the Jesus campaign that starts shortly after Satan begins the great tribulation, which could also occur on Day 1. If both begin on Day 1, then the rebellion in 2 Thessalonians would need to occur earlier in the first half of the seventieth week of Daniel. This then points to the fourth seal of Matthew 24:9 and Revelation 6:7–8 indicating a tribulation before Day 1. Therefore, there is a transition from a tribulation in the fourth opened seal to a great tribulation in the fifth opened seal.

FIGURE 15: FOURTH AND FIFTH OPENED SEALS (TRIBULATION AND GREAT TRIBULATION)

Matthew	2 Thessalonians	1 Timothy	Revelation
Tribulation and death (24:9)			Fourth opened seal: Death and famine (6:7–8)
Many fall away (24:10) Many false prophets (24:11)	Rebellion revealed before day of the Lord (2:3a) Man of lawlessness already at work (2:7)	"Some will depart from the faith" (4:1)	
Gospel proclaimed (24:14)			First angel proclaims eternal gospel (14:6–7) Third angel warns against worshiping the beast (14:9–11)
Those who endure will be saved (24:13)			Endurance of the saints (14:12)
Great tribulation (24:21) Abomination in the holy place (24:15)	Man of lawlessness seated in the temple (2:4) Restrained so "he may be revealed in his time" (2:6)		Fifth opened seal: martyrdom (6:9–11) Satan thrown to earth (12:7–12)

FIGURE 15: DISCUSSION OF COMMON THEMES

Each row of figure 15 shows a common motif revealed in multiple Scriptures during the fourth and fifth opened seals. It can be divided into three separate chronological segments. The first two rows cover the events in the fourth opened seal. The third and fourth rows reflect the warning from the three angels and the endurance of the saints just prior to the start of the fifth opened seal. The last row depicts the abomination of the temple, which begins the great tribulation and Jacob's trouble of the fifth opened seal.

The first row's common theme is tribulation and death. This is the topic in Matthew 24:9, which parallels Revelation 6:7–8, with the fourth opened seal unleashing death and famine.

The second row's common theme is the apostasy of the church. Matthew 24:10–11 says that "many will fall away" and "many false prophets will arise and lead many astray." 2 Thessalonians 2:3a speaks of a rebellion: "For that day will not come, unless the rebellion comes first." 2 Thessalonians 2:7a says, "For the mystery of lawlessness [man of lawlessness] is already at work." "Already at work" seems to refer to the man of lawlessness being active before Satan arrives on Day 1. "Only he [Michael] who now restrains it [Satan] will do so until he is out of the way" (2 Thess. 2:7b). The descriptions of the events in the first two rows point to the fourth opened seal lasting longer than a day. This would prevent the events from all occurring on Day 1. 1 Timothy 4:1a states the same thing: "Now the Spirit expressly says that in later times some will depart from the faith."

The events in the third row seems to occur at the end of the fourth opened seal. The first angel has proclaimed the gospel worldwide, which is associated with two Scriptures, Matthew 24:14 and Revelation 14:6–7. The third angel's warning in Revelation 14:9–11 is composed of two parts: First is the warning not to worship the beast and its image, and second is the warning not to take the mark of the beast. If both are done, the consequences are specified in Revelation 14:9–11.

The common theme in the next to last row is the endurance of the saints, spoken of in Matthew 24:13 and Revelation 14:12. The endurance of the saints is a reference to those who just lived through the fourth opened seal of tribulation and are now required to live through the opened fifth seal of the great tribulation.

The common theme of the last row relates to the revealing of the man of lawlessness, which starts the great tribulation with the fifth opened seal. Matthew 24:21 identifies this as the great tribulation. Parallel to this is the great wrath in Revelation 12:12. Both Matthew 24:21 and 2 Thessalonians 2:4 have the man of lawlessness in the holy place. Revelation 6:9–10 has the martyrdom of the saints.

FIFTH OPENED SEAL: MARTYRDOM AND THE GREAT TRIBULATION

Revelation 6:9–11 identifies the fifth opened seal as the martyrdom of those with the word of God. It parallels Matthew 24:15–26 where verse 21 identifies this as the great tribulation.

> For then there will be great tribulation, such as has not been from the beginning of the world until now, no, and never will be. And if those days had not been cut short, no human being would be saved. But for the sake of the elect those days will be cut short. (Matt. 24:21–22)

STRONGEST COUNTRIES DEALT WITH

At some point the man of lawlessness "shall *deal with* the strongest fortresses [countries] with the help of a foreign god [Satan]" (Dan. 11:39a, emphasis added). Since Satan will not arrive until Day 1 with the fifth opened seal, these countries will likely not be dealt with before then. This is commonly considered some kind of warfare event. This author's perspective is that this could also be interpreted as restricting wheat, barley, oil, and wine from nations because of their disobedience.

SIXTH OPENED SEAL: WRATH OF THE LAMB – SECOND DAY OF THE LORD

Revelation 6:12–17 identifies the sixth opened seal as the wrath of the Lamb. Below, we will see that the darkness of the sixth opened seal is a time for Christians to rejoice because of the end of the great tribulation and our soon to arrive Messiah!

Those hiding in the caves in Revelation 6:15–17 is considered the same event of Isaiah 2:6–21 where idols are thrown away. Since they are throwing away their idols we can logically assume they have the mark of the beast. They will later be brought low (v. 9), which is likely in the seventh opened seal when they return home. They were expecting calamity in the sixth opened seal though the seventh opened seal of planting, building, and marriages point to normal life events. What else could possibly bring them low is not specifically stated in Scripture. As a guess it could be related to vision related miracle before the first rapture, since when Jesus returns in the clouds every eye will see him (Revelation 1:7). See figure 16.

Those with the mark of the beast will experience the wrath of the Lamb. Isaiah 2:12–21 says this is the day of the Lord when they throw away their idols and are later brought low and humbled. The wicked throwing away their idols is a representation of the Antichrist temporarily losing control in Matthew 24:29 with the tribulation ending. This day of the Lord should be considered mild judgment for the wicked. It is certainly possible for death to occur from say a tsunami created from the great earthquake in Revelation 6:12, to those who live on any water coastline and fires from gas line breaks. Shortly later when the first trumpet is blown in Revelation 8:7 is when the destructive day of the Lord begins on earth with blood, fire, and hail.

> For the Lord of hosts has a day against all that is proud and lofty, against all that is lifted up—and it shall be brought low. (Isa. 2:12)

> And the idols shall utterly pass away. And people shall enter the caves of the rocks and the holes of the ground. (Isa. 2:18–19)

SEVENTH OPENED SEAL: NORMAL LIFE, THEN RAPTURE

Revelation 8:1–5 identifies the seventh opened seal. This author considers it parallel with Matthew 24:30–31, 37–42 and Luke 17:24–28. The seventh opened seal begins with darkness turning to light and ends some time on either the seventh or eighth day. This occurs with the "peals of thunder, rumblings, flashes of *lightning*, and an earthquake" of the first great eschatology theophany (Rev. 8:5b, emphasis added). It culminates with the resurrection and rapture of the church. And then Christ will return in the sky, as spoken of in Matthew 24:30–31, followed by the rapture. "He covers his hands with the *lightning* and commands it to strike the mark" (Job 36:32, emphasis added).

NO TRIBULATION WHEN THE SIXTH OR SEVENTH SEALS ARE OPENED

In this section, we will summarize the evidence that there is no tribulation when the sixth and seventh seals are opened. In the sixth opened seal there is the wrath of Lamb (wrath of God) for those have the mark of the beast.

As a consequence, those without the mark of the beast will no longer be in danger of being persecuted for their faith.

The association of Acts 2:17–21 with the "wrath of the Lamb" in the sixth opened seal was disproved in chapter 2. There, we showed that it should be associated with the Jehoshaphat Campaign of the sixth blown trumpet. Dispelling this moves us closer to understanding the truth about the meaning of the sixth and seventh opened seals.

In chapter 3, we saw that the rapture, the first great eschatological theophany, does not happen until the end of the seventh opened seal in Revelation 8:5. Also, the events in Revelation 7 do not chronologically occur until after this rapture though before Revelation 8:6 when the seven trumpets are issued. That is, the multitude in heaven from Revelation 7:9–17 is the consequence of the resurrection and rapture in Revelation 8:5. The 144,000 of Israel sealed in Revelation 7:1–8 also seems to be a consequence of Revelation 8:5.

Isaiah 2:9–12 says the Lord will bring proud and lofty people low. Verse 8 identifies these people as those who worship idols. When they flee to the caves in Isaiah 2:19, they carry their idols with them. That they would bring with them from their homes indicates a strong attachment to the idols. These people are likely those with the mark of the beast, who worship its image.

Figure 16 shows a series of events with parallel Scripture references. In the first row, the great tribulation ends when people throw away their idols during an event they call "the wrath of the Lamb." These individuals are those with the mark of the beast since earlier the beast of the earth "deceives those who dwell on earth, telling them to make an image for the beast that was wounded by the sword and yet lived" (Rev. 13:14b). When the rapture occurs, "two men will be in the field; one will be taken and one left" (Matt. 24:40). Also, "they were eating and drinking and marrying and being given in marriage, until the day when Noah entered the ark, and the flood came and destroyed them all" (Luke 17:27). These normal, everyday activities do not represent the wrath of the God, which scholars have occurring during the seventh opened seal. The reference to marriages occurring prior to the rapture is noteworthy. "Now the Spirit expressly says that in later [eschatological] times some will depart from the faith by devoting themselves to deceitful spirits and teachings of demons, through the insincerity of liars whose consciences are seared, who forbid marriage" (1 Tim. 4:1–3a). Departing from the faith is parallel to the rebellion in 2 Thessalonians 2:3a. Scripture seems to be indicating that these marriages just prior to the rapture are of those who fell away from the faith. By throwing away their idols earlier in the sixth open seal, they are now released from the control of the Antichrist, at least until they build idols again during the blown trumpets. Chapters 6 and 7 provide support that this falling away started prior to Day 1. These marriages may not be godly marriages between a man and a woman, though the point Scripture seems to be emphasizing is that there are now marriages, while previously there were likely none. Scripture does not, of course, restrict believers from getting married.

So we recognize that those getting married likely have the mark of the beast and, therefore, they can be identified as the people planting in Luke 17:26–28. The believers who just lived through the great tribulation would realize they would not be on earth long enough to enjoy the fruits of their labor from planting because, as discussed in chapter 3, the rapture occurs on either the seventh or eighth day of the seventh opened seal.

FIGURE 16: SIXTH AND SEVENTH OPENED SEALS (NO TRIBULATION)

Genesis and Isaiah	Matthew 24 and 1 Timothy 4	Luke and 2 Thessalonians	Revelation 6, 7, 8
Idols thrown away (Isa. 2:8–20)	Great tribulation ends (Matt. 24:29)	Sun, moon, and stars (darkness) (Luke 21:25)	Opened seal 6: Sun like sackcloth (darkness) (6:12)
The earth shaken (Isa. 2:19b)	Powers of heaven shaken (Matt. 24:29b)		Earthquake (6:12)
People flee to caves in the rocks (Isa. 2:19–21)			People hide in caves and among the rocks (6:15)
"For in seven days" (Gen. 7:4a)	Two men in a field (light) (Matt. 24:40)	Planting as in the days of Lot (light) (Luke 17:26–28)	Opened seal 7: Half an hour of silence in heaven (7.5 days) (see figure 5; 8:1)
	Marriages forbidden earlier (1 Tim. 4:1–3)	Marriages again before wrath of God (Luke 17:27b)	
Rain for forty days and forty nights (wrath) (Gen. 7:4b)	One man taken and one left behind (Matt. 24:40)	Rapture and wrath on same day (Luke 17:27–30)	144,000 sealed and multitude in heaven (ch. 7). Rapture (8:5) followed by wrath (8:6ff.)
		Lightning flashes—Son of man (Luke 17:24–26)	Lightning flashes in theophany (8:5)

ISRAEL AND THE CHURCH SET FREE FROM EXILE WITH THE SIXTH OPENED SEAL

As discussed in chapter 3, the great tribulation ends at the start of the sixth opened seal and continues into the seventh opened seal. Those previously being persecuted for their faith include both the church and Israel. We know that when the sixth seal is opened, there is a great earthquake in Revelation 6:12. Scripturally, at that moment, those being persecuted for their faith could have their restraints removed. It seems similar to when the persecuted apostle Paul was unrestrained after a great earthquake.

> Suddenly there was a great earthquake, so that the foundations of the prison were shaken. And immediately all the doors were opened, and everyone's bonds were unfastened. (Acts 16:26)

The church would be raptured in Revelation 8:5 with the first great theophany before the destructive wrath of God in the blown trumpets. Since Israel will not be raptured until Day 1,260, it seems Israel will have at least 34 to 40 days (sixth and seventh opened seal duration) to leave their exile locations and make their way to safety. After this, the wicked would be expected to start building idols and worshiping them again, as noted later during the blown trumpets. We recognize this with the sixth blown trumpet of Revelation 9:20–21. With idols being worshiped again it indicates anyone without the mark of the beast and who does not worship his image is again in danger of persecution.

An analogy can be made with their Egyptian historical exile. Their exile departure date (day after Nisan 15 in Ex. 12) until they arrived in the Sinai wilderness was about 44 days (new moon of Sivan 1 in Ex. 19:1). Exodus 19:2 points to some amount of time to travel from Rephidim to their encampment location at the base of Mt. Sinai. This travel time could be the reason for about four missing days. Perhaps when they entered the wilderness of Sinai, after about the forty days, they were considered safe from harm.

FALSE SECURITY OF THOSE WITH THE MARK OF BEAST

Even though the people on earth will have experienced the great tribulation and its terror, those with the mark of the beast will be humbled afterwards only temporarily. They will still have their consciences seared. "Now the Spirit expressly says that in later times some will depart from the faith by devoting themselves to deceitful spirits and teachings of demons, through the insincerity of liars whose consciences are seared" (1 Tim. 4:1–2). When the seventh seal is opened, those who worship the beast and its image and have the mark will go about doing their regular activities with a false sense of security before the wrath of God. They will eat, drink, plant, build, and live life without concern, as Jesus predicted in Luke 17:26–30. Those who have not fallen away from their faith should recognize that the rapture would occur soon and they would not be on the earth long enough to enjoy the fruits of their labor by planting and building. Since there is no reference to the use of oil lamps to perform these outdoor activities, we have to assume they are during light. We now recognize the contrast between the twenty-four darkness of the sixth opened seal (Rev. 6:11–17) and the light of the seventh opened seal (Luke 17:26–30).

After the end of the great tribulation, it will be safe for Christians to travel out. Though because of the chaos of those with the mark of the beast from the "wrath of the Lamb" and darkness of the sixth opened seal, we may want to wait until the daylight of the opened seventh seal. The chaos would likely include them quickly finding a place to hid in rocks and caves. If this is interpreted literally, then many would be generally be traveling to mountains. This higher elevation destination could be a consequence of tsunamis from the great earthquake of Revelation 6:12. Buying and selling in Luke 17:28 would be expected with the daylight of the opened seventh seal. Having just lived through the great tribulation, some Christians may still feel threatened being around those with the mark of the beast, though we should not. In fact, the Lord takes it a step further: "So man is humbled, and each one is brought low—do not forgive them!" (Isa. 2:9).

COINS AND WITNESSING

So Christians who have a medical need or lack food may need to find a business or nearby neighbor with the mark who would be willing to accept silver or gold coins or just barter to purchase something. Considering the rapture will occur on the seventh or eighth day of the seventh opened seal, there will be no need to be thrifty. In fact, we may want to overpay to get the service that day or the next day since we will no longer be on earth in less than nine days. The emotional challenge would be recognizing that those who have taken the mark of the beast and worship the beast and his image are doomed to the eternal wrath of God. It does not even seem possible to witness and spiritually save them since God gave them a strong delusion in 2 Thessalonians 2:9–11. However, while they feel perfectly safe, the wrath of God—sudden destruction—will come upon them, and they will not escape it.

> The coming of the lawless one is by the activity of Satan with all power and false signs and wonders, and with all wicked deception for those who are perishing, because they refused to love the truth and so be saved. Therefore God sends them a strong delusion, so that they may believe what is false. (2 Thess. 2:9–11)

> Just as it was in the days of Noah, so will it be in the days of the Son of Man. They were eating and drinking and marrying and being given in marriage, until the day when Noah entered the ark, and the flood came and destroyed them all. Likewise, just as it was in the days of Lot—they were eating and drinking, buying and selling, *planting and building* [light activities], but on the day when Lot went out from Sodom, fire and sulfur rained from heaven and destroyed them all—so will it be on the day when the Son of Man is revealed. (Luke 17:26–30, emphasis added)

> For you yourselves are fully aware that the day of the Lord will come like a thief in the night. While people are saying, "There is peace and security," then sudden destruction will come upon them as labor pains come upon a pregnant woman, and they will not escape. (1 Thess. 5:2–3)

FALSE CHRISTS (PROPHETS) CAUSE REBELLION

The prophecy in 2 Thessalonians 2:3–4 warns us to not be deceived even prior to Day 1.

> Let no one deceive you in any way. For that day (first day of the Lord) will not come, unless the rebellion [NKJV, "falling away"] comes first, and the man of lawlessness is revealed, the son of destruction, who opposes and exalts himself against every so-called god or object of worship, so that he takes his seat in the temple of God, proclaiming himself to be God. (2 Thess. 2:3–4)

In the Olivet Discourse in Matthew 24:4–5, 11, 23, Jesus warns us three separate times to beware of false christs. The warnings are when the first, fourth, and fifth seals are opened. These false prophets will lead many away from the faith who were enlightened and saw that the Lord is good by the power of the Holy Spirit but were never "owned" by Him.

> For the time is coming when people will not endure sound teaching, but having itching ears they will accumulate for themselves teachers to suit their own passions, and will turn away from listening to the truth and wander off into myths. As for you, always be sober-minded, endure suffering, do the work of an evangelist, fulfill your ministry. (2 Tim. 4:3–5)

FIGURE 17: BEYOND PREWRATH OVERVIEW TIMELINE

◄——— 3½ years ———►		Great		
Birth pangs	Tribulation	tribulation	No	Wrath
Opened	Opened	Opened	tribulation	of God
seals 1–3	seal 4	seal 5	Opened ▲	
Matt. 24:4–8	Matt. 24:9–14	Matt. 24:15–26	seals	Rev.
Rev. 6:1–6	Rev. 6:7–8	Rev. 6:9–11	6 and 7	8:6ff.
Beware of false christs			34–40	
Matthew 24:4–5, 11, 23–26			days	

Day 1   Rapture
                                   Rev. 8:5;
                                   then
                                   Rev. 7

FIFTH OPENED SEAL ON DAY 1

Most scholars have three or four opened seals located in the first half of the seventieth week of Daniel. My position is that there are four, which is supported by the following:

The first step to understand this is to ask when the abomination of desolation in the Jerusalem temple occurs. Daniel 9:27 says it will occur in the middle of the seventieth week of Daniel (Day 1). Matthew 24:15 references this Daniel abomination of desolation. These events are therefore the same event.

And he shall make a strong covenant with many for one week, and for half of the week he shall put an end to sacrifice and offering. And on the wing of *abominations shall come one who makes desolate*, until the decreed end is poured out on the desolator. (Dan. 9:27, emphasis added)

So when you see the *abomination of desolation* spoken of by the prophet Daniel, standing in the holy place (let the reader understand), then let those who are in Judea flee to the mountains. (Matt. 24:15, emphasis added)

The earlier Matthew 24:15–26 parallel to Revelation 6:9–11 in figure 12 was shown to be in the fifth opened seal. Therefore, the fifth opened seal seems to start on Day 1 and, correspondingly, the first four opened seals occurring in the first half of the seventieth week of Daniel.

FIRST TRUMPET BLOWN: WRATH OF GOD

Revelation 8:6–7 describes the preparation to sound the trumpets and then the sounding of the first trumpet. The first trumpet will bring hail and fire mixed with blood, the start of the destruction of the earth. It will parallel Noah and Lot in Matthew 24:37–42 and Luke 17:26–30.

CONCLUSION

The great tribulation will end at the start of the sixth opened seal (Isa. 2:18, 20; Matt. 24:29; Rev. 6:12). Those with the mark of beast will suffer the wrath of the Lamb where they are expecting total destruction though later they are brought low. This wrath of God should be considered mild to insignificant considering the wrath to come with the blown trumpets and poured bowls. The sixth and seventh opened seals have no tribulation, which means those without the mark of the beast will be safe to go about their normal business without danger of persecution from those with the mark of the beast, though may want to wait until after the chaos and darkness of the opened sixth seal ends. Although, if there is a miracle during the sixth opened to bring those with the mark of the beast low (Isa. 2:9; Rev. 1:7), then that would provide confidence for Christians to venture out into the darkness for critical supplies.

The first four opened seals appear to occur in the first half of the seventieth week of Daniel. The fourth opened seal is identified with tribulation and death. Matthew 24:9 parallels Revelation 6:7–8, describing the fourth opened seal bringing death and famine. Many false prophets arising in Matthew 24:11 appears to begin the falling away of the church. This timing of the apostasy is confirmed in 2 Thessalonians 2:2–3, which has it occurring before the day of the Lord. The first eschatological day of the Lord likely occurs on Day 1, as supported in the chapter 2. Then, the tribulation will get worse, becoming the great tribulation of Matthew 24:21. The great tribulation begins with the fifth opened seal. From Revelation 12 we recognize that Satan is thrown to the earth on Day 1.

Chapter 7

The Eschatological Day of the Lord: About Day 1

PURPOSE

Current scholarly interpretation concerning when the eschatological day of the Lord will occur varies. Many say the wrath of God is equivalent to the day of the Lord. Others say the day of the Lord includes only Armageddon, during the sixth poured bowl. This chapter and the next present a different view that there are seven separate eschatological day of the Lord events. This chapter will examine the attack by Gog and Jesus's counter attack in Israel. Chapter 8 will discuss the remaining eschatological day of the Lord events. This chapter and the next do not necessarily contain a complete list of all eschatological day of the Lord and Christ events, though enough to prove the purpose.

ESCHATOLOGICAL WRATH OF GOD

Many scholars incorrectly use the eschatological wrath of God and the eschatological day of the Lord interchangeably. There are seven separate eschatological days of the Lord. There are at least three separate general chronological components of the eschatological wrath of God depending on how one groups them. The first eschatological day of the Lord and the associated wrath of God occur when the Lord responds in anger against Gog, as described in event 6. As discussed in chapter 6, the second day of the Lord (wrath of the Lamb) in the sixth open seal is not representative as physical death (Isa. 2:12–21 and Rev. 6:12–17).

The third general eschatological wrath of God will occur after each trumpet is blown and each bowl is poured. This is supported by Revelation 16:1, which says that the wrath of God includes the seven poured bowls, and Revelation 15:1, which says that the wrath will be completed with the upcoming poured bowls. So the wrath of God will start before the bowls are poured. In chapter 3, we saw that the rapture in Revelation 8:5 immediately precedes the wrath of God in Revelation 8:6ff. There will be no tribulation when the sixth and seventh seals are opened. After the rapture of the elect

(Revelation 8:5) the wrath of God will begin (Revelation 8:7) on the entire earth. We know "God has not destined us for wrath, but to obtain salvation through our Lord Jesus Christ" (1 Thess. 5:9). These reasons support the second eschatological wrath of God occurring in Revelation 8:6ff.

> Then I saw another sign in heaven, great and amazing, seven angels with seven plagues, which are the last, for with them the *wrath of God* is finished. (Rev. 15:1, emphasis added)

> Then I heard a loud voice from the temple telling the seven angels, "Go and pour out on the earth the seven bowls of the *wrath of God*." (Rev. 16:1, emphasis added)

TWO WITNESSES ARRIVE JUST BEFORE SATAN

Two witnesses will arrive several days before Satan empowers the man of lawlessness, becoming the Antichrist on Day 1. On this day the two witnesses, false prophet, as well as Jesus, will be able to call fire from heaven (Zech. 14:3–13; Rev. 11:5; 13:13).

DAY 1: SIX BASIC EVENTS

Several unique events begin on or about Day 1, as shown chronologically in figure 18. Some events can be expected to last only a few moments, such as event 3 (the proclamation by three angels), and some to last much longer, such as event 4 (the persecution by the Antichrist (Gog) and his ten king coalition). Several of these events can be expected to overlap. The following observations can help in understanding the chronology of these events.

- Jesus likely will leave heaven for earth before Satan and his angels are unrestrained in heaven and then thrown to earth. Scripture makes no reference to Jesus being in heaven during the battle of Revelation 12. The residents of Jerusalem also appear to be on their rooftops a bit before the temple abomination. This seems to require Jesus to arrive on earth before Satan is thrown to earth.

- Jesus warned, "So when you see the abomination of desolation spoken of by the prophet Daniel, standing in the holy place (let the reader understand), then let those who are in Judea flee to the mountains. Let the one who is on the housetop not go down to take what is in his house" (Matt. 24:15–17). Since the residents of Jerusalem are expected to be on their rooftops when the valley is formed during event 1, it seems reasonable to assume the events that cause them to flee are the proclamations of the angels of event 3, followed shortly by the Antichrist's abomination of event 4.

- "For the mystery of lawlessness is already at work. Only he who now restrains it will do so until he is out of the way. And then the lawless one will be revealed" (2 Thess. 2:7–8a). The restrainer will be shown to be the archangel Michael. Also, it seems the one being restrained is Satan and possibly his angels in heaven. After he is released, there will be a battle in heaven, and Satan and his angels will be thrown to earth. When on earth, Satan will enter the man of lawlessness and become the Antichrist. The temple abomination will likely occur on that same day. If this analysis is correct, then the heavenly battle of event 2 will occur prior to the attack on Israel and persecution by the Antichrist of event 4.

- "But on that day, the day that Gog shall come against the land of Israel, declares the Lord GOD, my wrath will be roused in my anger" (Ezek. 38:18). That day is the Jerusalem campaign (Zech. 14:3–5), probably on or shortly after Day 1. Therefore, the Lord's counterattack (event 6) must occur after the Antichrist's attack (event 4).

FIGURE 18: CHRONOLOGY OF ESCHATOLOGICAL EVENTS
AROUND DAY 1

Two witnesses arrive on earth at least a few days before Day 1	Mal. 4:5; Rev. 11:3, 9–12

Event 1: Jesus visits Mount of Olives	Isa. 29:5–7

Event 2 in heaven	
a. Michael's restraining of dragon ends	Dan. 12:1
b. War begins	Rev. 12:7–8
c. Dragon and his angels thrown to earth	Rev. 12:9

Events 3–6 on earth	
3. Three angel proclamations	Rev. 14:6–11
4. Antichrist in the temple, then persecution	Zech. 14:1–2
5. Israel flees; Archangel Michael protects the Jewish remnant for 1,260 days	Rev. 12:6, 13–14
6. First day of the Lord	Zech. 14:3–13

EVENT 1: JESUS VISITS MOUNT OF OLIVES

Jesus's visit will likely begin at Bethany, with Jesus then moving northwest toward the Mount of Olives. We know Jesus will return the way he left from Acts 1:11: "Men of Galilee, why do you stand looking into heaven? This Jesus, who was taken up from you into heaven, will come in the same way as you saw him go into heaven." The location of Jesus's eschatological return will be where He left them: "And he led them out as far as Bethany, and lifting up his hands he blessed them. While he blessed them, he parted from them and was carried up into heaven" (Luke 24:50–51). Jesus's return to Jerusalem is described clearly: "On that day his feet will stand on the Mount of Olives that lies before Jerusalem on the east, and the Mount of Olives shall be split in two from east to west by a very wide valley, so that one half of the Mount shall move northward, and the other half southward" (Zech. 14:4). The mountains being moved are expected to be a consequence of the great earthquake of Ezekiel 38:19, shortly later likely when Gog attacks Israel.

So this wide valley will be aligned from the temple mount (the expected location of the future third temple) toward the east. Zechariah has Jesus's feet standing on the Mount of Olives. Therefore, Jesus's eschatological return appears to be at Bethany, and then He will make his way toward the Mount of Olives.

The impression from Scripture is that the residents in Jerusalem will have enough time to get to their rooftops and observe the action to the east for at least a short amount of time. This amount of time would allow for Jesus to make his way north west over the mountainous terrain from Bethany to the Mount of Olives. The Bible does not seem to say how Jesus will make his way from Bethany to the Mount of Olives, though it could be by walking or on a cloud. When Jesus arrives at the Mount of Olives and the valley is formed, this becomes the escape route for the Jews. "And you shall flee to the valley of my mountains, for the valley of the mountain shall reach to Azal" (Zech. 14:5a).

FLIGHT OF THE RESIDENTS OF JERUSALEM

Isaiah 29:6 seems to describe the first eschatological return: "you will be visited by the LORD of hosts with thunder and with earthquake and great noise, with whirlwind and tempest and the flame of a devouring fire." Jesus is "visiting," which indicates a short amount of time. Thunder is normally associated with dark clouds and a lack of sunlight, so this appears to be the same theophany as Zechariah 14:7: "a unique day, which is known to the LORD, neither day nor night, but at evening time there shall be light." This same event is where "every wall shall tumble to the ground" (Ezek. 38:20b), likely from "a great earthquake in the land of Israel" (Ezek. 38:19b).

As this theophany unfolds, many in Jerusalem will go to their rooftops to see this with their own eyes. Since the Mount of Olives is about a mile east of Jerusalem, this would make for a spectacular once-in-a-lifetime event. Depending on the perspective of those on their rooftops, it is possible that their "eyes will behold the king [Jesus] in his beauty; they will see a land that stretches afar" (Isa. 33:17). This far-off land is probably the mountains of the Jordan. This location being safety for the Jewish remnant has merit since Edom, Moab, and the Ammonites will be out of the Antichrist control (Dan. 11:41). Isaiah's parallel prophecy says, "The oracle concerning the valley of vision. What do you mean that you have gone up, all of you, to the housetops?" (Isa. 22:1).

Jesus warned us about this: "So when you see the abomination of desolation spoken of by the prophet Daniel, standing in the holy place (let the reader understand), then let those who are in Judea flee to the mountains. Let the one who is on the housetop not go down to take what is in his house" (Matt. 24:15–17). Since "Jerusalem shall remain aloft on its site" (Zech. 14:10b), the residents will feel secure when looking to the east at the valley forming. Since they are expected to be on their rooftops when event 1 begins, it is reasonable to assume the proclamation of the angels (event 3) and the Antichrist's abomination (event 4) must come shortly later, while they are still on their rooftops. Jesus's instructions to flee to the mountains in Matthew 24:15–17 is equivalent to Zechariah 14:5a: "And you shall flee to the valley of my mountains, for the valley of the mountains shall reach to Azal." Those Jews fleeing to the east are the only ones on earth who are protected from persecution for 1,260 days (Rev. 12:6, 13–17).

JESUS LEAVES HEAVEN BEFORE HEAVENLY BATTLE

It appears that the persecution of event 4 will begin shortly after the dragon (Satan) and his angels are hurled to earth from heaven on Day 1 (Rev. 12:7–8). Jesus and his holy ones will respond to the persecution with event 6, and event 5 will provide a means of escape for the Jews (Zech. 14:5). Imagine the spiritual battle scene in heaven when everyone leaves on the same day, with all that fury being brought initially to Israel and then the world! Since Jesus is not mentioned in the heavenly battle in Revelation 12:7–12, He probably arrived on earth earlier.

FIGURE 19: JESUS'S VISIT AND JERUSALEM CAMPAIGN

Isaiah	Ezekiel	Zechariah	Matthew and Jeremiah
The Lord visits Jerusalem; earthquake, great noise, whirlwind, and fire (event 1) (22:10, 21; 29:6)	Earthquake in Israel causes every wall to fall (38:19–20)	Earthquake, but Jerusalem remains aloft (14:4–5, 10)	
Thunder (implies dark clouds) (29:6)		Neither day nor night (implies dark clouds) (14:7)	
All on their housetops and see a land that stretches afar (22:1; 33:17b)		Very wide valley formed (event 1) (14:4)	On their housetops (Matt. 24:17)
See the King in his beauty (22:17a)		Jesus on Mount of Olives (event 1) (14:4)	
Weeping and mourning; thrown into wide land (22:12; 17–18)	Gog attacks Israel and seizes plunder (event 3) (14:14–18; 38:13)	Plunder divided and half the city into exile (14:1, 2b)	Jacob's trouble (Jer. 30:7)
		Flee to the mountain valley (event 4) (14:5a)	Flee without going into the house (flee) (Matt. 24:15–17)
"In that day"; people burned to lime (22:25; 33:12, 16)	Plague and bloodshed against Gog, turning them against each other (38:21–23)	Lord fighting on that day (event 5) (14:3)	

EVENT 2: ARCHANGEL MICHAEL HAS MANY ROLES

The archangel Michael has several different roles during these events.

Michael first appears as a protective chief prince: "The prince of the kingdom of Persia withstood me twenty-one days, but Michael, one of the chief princes, came to help me" (Dan. 10:13a). So one of prince Michael's roles is a celestial (heavenly) rescuer.

During the war in heaven, Michael will lead his angels in defeating the dragon (Satan) and his angels and throwing them to earth (Rev. 12:7–9). As a consequence, "the devil has come down to you in great wrath, because he knows that his time is short" (Rev. 12:12b). Revelation 12:13–17 describes Satan pursuing the woman (Israel) and then her offspring (the church). Then Satan begins his three and a half years of persecution on earth. Therefore, Michael is in heaven when the heavenly battle begins. Also, these events place the war in heaven on Day 1.

Finally, "at that time shall arise Michael, the great prince who has charge of your people. And there shall be a time of trouble, such as never has been since there was a nation till that time. But at that time your people shall be delivered" (Dan. 12:1a). This time of trouble refers to the second half of the seventieth week of Daniel, also called Jacob's trouble. A case can be made that Jacob's trouble begins when the fourth seal is opened with world persecution. Since Daniel was Jewish, "your people" are the Jewish tribes. This parallels the story of the dragon and the woman in Revelation 12:13–16.

EVENT 2: WHO IS THE RESTRAINER AND WHO IS BEING RESTRAINED?

For many centuries, scholars have debated who the restrainer in 2 Thessalonians 2:6–7 is. Some say the restrainer is the Holy Spirit, Satan, the archangel Michael, or the government. The following evidence supports the idea that the restrainer is Michael and the ones being restrained are Satan and his angels in heaven.

Daniel 12:1 says that Michael will arise, or "stand up" (NKJV). Many scholars interpret Michael standing up as getting out of the way. But when war breaks out in heaven, it is Michael who takes the lead to throw Satan and all his angels from heaven to earth. None of his roles give the impression that Michael is not taking action by standing up. So it seems that this must be interpreted differently.

During the first half of the seventieth week of Daniel, the man of lawlessness on earth is not restrained. In fact, the man of lawlessness is likely causing the tribulation and death of the fourth opened seal. In chapter 5 we deduced that the little horn was causing the peaceful conquest of the first opened seal. During the battle in heaven in Revelation 12, Satan and his angels are thrown to earth on Day 1.

When the battle of Revelation 12:7 begins, the archangel Michael and his angels as well as Satan and all of his angels are in heaven. Having all the angels in heaven at the same moment seems highly unusual, especially considering Day 1 is a historic eschatological event when the temple will be desecrated (Dan. 9:27). Why would some not be roaming the earth? We know from Job 1:7 that Satan roamed the earth. Satan also was on earth when he tempted Jesus (Matt. 4:1–11). Might Satan be held against his will in heaven until it is time for the fulfillment of the eschatology prophecy (Jacob's trouble and the great tribulation)? That is, could Michael "standing up" be a metaphor for him releasing Satan and probably his angels from their restraints in heaven?

Adding strength to this interpretation is that when Satan is thrown out of heaven in Revelation 12 he chases the woman (Israel) though she is protected for 1,260 days. Israel will be shown to be raptured on Day 1,260 in Revelation 11:19. This points to Satan being thrown out of heaven on Day 1. If Satan roamed the earth prior to Day 1, then the fourth opened seal (Matt. 24:9–14; Rev. 6:7–8) would not be called the tribulation but the great tribulation. Instead, the great tribulation is in Matthew 24:15–26, which is parallel to the fifth opened seal of Revelation 6:9–11. So we know Satan arrives on earth on Day 1, which leads to the possibility that Satan is restrained in heaven prior to the fourth opened seal and likely well before the start of the seventieth week of Daniel. So it appears the ones restrained in 2 Thessalonians 2:6 are Satan and his angels, and Michael is the one restraining them until Day 1 of the heavenly battle.

FIGURE 20: SATAN ON DAY 1

Event (Day 1)	Daniel	Revelation
War in Heaven	Michael arises and a time of trouble (with Satan unrestrained) (12:1a)	War in heaven with dragon and his angels (12:7–8)
Satan thrown to earth		Beast rises out of the sea (12:12; 13:1).
Jacob's trouble (Jer. 30:7)	Michael has charge of the Jews during a time of trouble; deliverance of those found in the book (of life) (12:1)	12:13, 15 Satan pursues the woman (remnant of Israel), who flees and is nourished for 1,260 days (12:6, 13, 15)
Great tribulation (Matt. 24:21)	Destruction of mighty men and the saints (8:24b)	Fifth opened seal: Satan makes war against the woman's offspring (church) (6:9–11; 12:17)

EVENT 3: MESSAGES OF THE THREE ANGELS

Three angels make worldwide proclamations in Revelation 14:6–11. These proclamations are likely to occur while the residents of Jerusalem are still on their rooftops. This author considers this to be the last event of the fourth opened seal.

The endurance of the saints in Revelation 14:12 seems to point to enduring the great tribulation in Matthew 24:13. Interpreting Revelation 14:6–13 on Day 1 seems to have merit since the saints are later raptured in the seventh opened seal. In fact, Revelation 12:10b has the endurance of the saints starting when the dragon is thrown out of heaven. The endurance of the saints seems to also parallel Matthew 24:13, just after the third angel warning. This helps to support the three angel warnings on Day 1.

Those who fall away from their faith in 2 Thessalonians 2:2–5 was earlier shown to be prior to Day 1. There is no reference to falling away from the faith on or after Day 1.

But the one who endures to the end will be saved. (Matt. 24:13)

Here is a call for the endurance of the saints, those who keep the commandments of God and their faith in Jesus. (Rev. 14:12)

EVENT 4: PERSECUTION BY ANTICHRIST AND TEN NATIONS STARTS DAY 1

Event 4 is when the great tribulation of the church and Jacob's trouble for the Jewish people begin with the fifth opened seal on Day 1. Israel will experience a final eschatological exile and chastisement, though compared to historic experiences, it will be relatively brief, less than 1,260 days. The Egyptian exile lasted about four hundred years. The Babylonian exile lasted seventy years. The final eschatological Jewish exile will be different from all the others in that Israel will accept Jesus as their Messiah, become spiritually saved, and then later be raptured.

The man of lawlessness and a ten-nation coalition will attack Israel beginning on Day 1, if not moments before. "And the ten horns that you saw are ten kings who have not yet received royal power, but they are to receive authority as kings for one hour, together with the beast [the man of lawlessness]" (Rev. 17:12). "So when you see the abomination of desolation spoken of by the prophet Daniel, standing in the holy place (let the reader understand), then let those who are in Judea flee to the mountains" (Matt. 24:15–16). Many in Israel will be captured or killed, the empowered man of lawlessness (Antichrist) will desecrate the third temple, and there will be massive death in Israel. Zechariah 14:1–2 describes this massive persecution. Zechariah 14:5a is likely concurrent on Day 1: "You shall flee to the valley of my mountains, for the valley of the mountains shall reach to Azal." From Revelation 12:13–17 we see the dragon [Satan] will pursue the woman [Israel], though unsuccessfully. Those who escape to the east through the wide valley are the only ones on earth who are promised protection during this time of worldwide persecution.

SOME JEWS RETURN TO ISRAEL BEFORE DAY 1?

In Matthew 24:9 Jesus speaks of tribulation, which is persecution, and death. About twenty-eight percent of all Jews in the world live in Israel. This author believes the persecution and death of the fourth opened seal will cause some Jews to return to Israel to avoid this, though on Day 1 that will become the epicenter of Jacob's trouble. "Two thirds shall be cut off and perish, and one third shall be left alive" (Zech. 13:8b).

TEN KINGS AND THE BEAST ATTACK BABYLON

The ten kings attacking Babylon represents them carrying out God's purpose in Revelation 17:16–17.

> And the ten horns that you saw, they and the beast will hate the prostitute. They will make her desolate and naked, and devour her flesh and burn her up with fire, for God has put it into their hearts to carry out his purpose by being of one mind and handing over their royal power to the beast, until the words of God are fulfilled.

FIGURE 21: BABYLON ATTACKED

Isaiah 13	Zechariah 14	Revelation
Babylon attacked (v. 19)	Surrounding plains (vv. 5, 10)	Fallen is Babylon (14:8)
Earthquake (v. 13)	Earthquake (vv. 4–5)	
Sun dark at its rising (v. 10)	Neither night nor day. Light in the evening. (vv. 6–7)	
Death (vv. 15–16)		The prostitute (Babylon) fallen/ destroyed (14:8; 17:16–17)
Day of the Lord (v. 6)	Day of the Lord (v. 1)	Hour of judgment (14:7)

EVENT 5: MICHAEL, PROTECTOR OF GOD'S PEOPLE

"But at that time your people shall be delivered, everyone whose name shall be found written in the book" (Dan. 12:1b). This deliverance refers to a Jewish remnant being protected from this time of trouble in Revelation 12:6, 13–17. This has a duration of 1,260 days (three and a half years), which is considered to be the duration of Jacob's trouble for the Jewish people.

After the dragon [Satan] is thrown to earth, it pursues the woman [Israel], though she is protected and nourished for three and a half years (Rev. 12:13–17). Day 1 appears to be when Satan is thrown to earth. "At that time shall arise Michael, the great prince who has charge of your people" (Dan. 12:1a). The NKJV Bible translation says "who stands watch over the sons of your people" Michael also has a special responsibility to care for the nation of Israel (Dan. 10:13–14, 21). So who will be specifically protected? The answer is found in Daniel 12:1b: "And there shall be a time of trouble, such as never has been since there was a nation till that time. But at that time your people shall be delivered, everyone whose name shall be found written in the book." This "time of trouble" refers to Jacob's trouble in Jeremiah 30:7. Since Daniel was Jewish, "your people" refers to the Jewish tribes. Though a remnant will be protected and nourished for 1,260 days, many others will go into exile. "Though the number of the sons of Israel be as the sand of the sea, only a remnant of them will be saved" (Rom. 9:27). Therefore, Revelation 12:14 could describe Michael's second mission, to protect the remnant of Israel during Jacob's trouble.

PHARISEES AND SADDUCEES FLEE BEFORE THE WRATH

I find John the Baptist's greeting of the Pharisees and Sadducees interesting (when he was at the Jordan river baptizing believers—Matt. 3:7): "You brood of vipers! Who warned you to flee from the wrath to come?" He first accused them of being, metaphorically, a den of poisonous snakes, though he gave them credit for fleeing the wrath to come.

Why would he give them credit for fleeing Jerusalem, and what wrath to come could he have been thinking of? John surely knew he was the prophet (Mal. 3:1; 4:5–6) who prepared the way before the Lord. After his death (Matt. 14:1–12), we learn that John the Baptist was a type of Elijah, as described in Matthew 17:10–13. John's greeting to the Pharisees and Sadducees indicates he was thinking the eschatological wrath of God might occur shortly, with the epicenter being Israel, especially Jerusalem. John the Baptist was not alone among first century believers in thinking the eschatological day of the Lord might begin shortly. Even about two or three decades later, believers with the apostle Paul (in 2 Thess. 2:1–5) asked him whether the day of the Lord had begun (see chapter 2).

John was certainly familiar with Zechariah 14:1–13's eschatological day of the Lord in Jerusalem, when the Jews escape the abomination of desolation at the Temple Mount toward the east, where the mountains of the Mount of Olives once were. The Jordan river is on the eastern border of Israel, which will be the general eschatological escape route of the Jewish remnant as described in Zechariah 14:4–5. This remnant are the only ones on earth who will miraculously be protected from the persecution of the Antichrist during the great tribulation (Rev. 12:13–17).

TWO WITNESSES

"And I will grant authority to my two witnesses, and they will prophesy for 1,260 days, clothed in sackcloth" (Rev. 11:3). As discussed in chapter 2, the two witnesses are expected to arrive several days before Day 1. We also know only the remnant of Israel will be protected and nourished for 1,260 days, starting on Day 1 (Rev. 12:14). These two witnesses from heaven will do signs and wonders and "strike the earth with every kind of plague, as often as they desire" (Rev. 11:6). They will testify to the power of the God to those on earth during that time. The two are completely supernaturally protected until they finish with their testimony. "And if anyone would harm them, fire pours from their mouth and consumes their foes. If anyone would harm them, this is how he is doomed to be killed" (Rev. 11:5). "And when they have finished their testimony, the beast that rises from the bottomless pit will make war on them and conquer them and kill them" (Rev. 11:7).

EVENT 6: FIRST DAY OF THE LORD AND JERUSALEM CAMPAIGN

The Jerusalem campaign is the first of Jesus's three eschatological military campaigns. This is the day of the Lord (Zech. 14:1).[1] The same day of the Lord is described in 2 Thessalonians 2:2b. It is the first known eschatological day of the Lord, as summarized in figures 22 and 27. "But on that day, the day that Gog shall come against the land of Israel, declares the Lord GOD, my wrath will be roused in my anger" (Ezek. 38:18). The Lord's anger being roused causes the start of the first eschatological day of the Lord. "Then the LORD will go out and fight against those nations as when he fights on a day of battle" (Zech. 14:3). The Lord's attack against those who are waging war in Jerusalem is described in Zechariah 14:12 as a plague where "their

---

1   See figure 19.

flesh will rot while they are still standing on their feet, their eyes will rot in their sockets, and their tongues will rot in their mouths." Since Gog attacks first (event 4) and the Lord responds (event 6), the Lord's response could be called a counterattack. "On that day there shall be no light, cold, or frost. And there shall be a unique day, which is known to the LORD, neither day nor night" (Zech. 14:6–7a).

The Jerusalem campaign of Jesus does not stop the persecution of event 4, though it would be expected to temporally pause it or temporally slow it down. "But at evening time there shall be light" (Zech. 14:7b).

BROTHER AGAINST BROTHER (FRATRICIDE)

"I will summon a sword against Gog on all my mountains, declares the Lord GOD. Every man's sword will be against his brother. With pestilence and bloodshed I will enter into judgment with him, and I will rain upon him and his hordes and the many peoples who are with him torrential rains and hailstones, fire and sulfur" (Ezek. 38:21–22). Each brother attacking his brother should not be a surprise for the following reasons: First, Genesis 16:11–12 prophesies that Ishmael's hand will be against everyone and everyone's hand against him. Second, the eschatological analogy to this expected internal strife seems to represent "the kingdom [that] shall be partly strong and partly brittle" (Dan. 2:42b).

> And on that day a great panic from the LORD shall fall on them, so that each will seize the hand of another, and the hand of the one will be raised against the hand of the other. (Zech. 14:13)

"ALL NATIONS" HYPERBOLE

"For I will gather all the nations against Jerusalem to battle" (Zech. 14:2a). "All nations" refers to Gog and his coalition, as discussed in Ezekiel 38:21–22. This is not a reference to all nations in the world, only the Antichrist and the ten kings. We know from Daniel 9:26 that wars will continue to the end, therefore not all nations will be conquered. Chapter 2 describes other similar examples of hyperbole.

REVEALING THE MAN OF LAWLESSNESS

The revealing of the man of lawlessness appears to be chronologically bound to Day 1 for the following reasons:[2]

As shown earlier in the discussion of event 2, the archangel Michael in Daniel 12:1 seems to be standing up to release Satan from his restraints in heaven. From Revelation 12:7–8 the release date seems to be timed to Day 1 to fulfill prophecy (the start of the great tribulation and Jacob's trouble). From this then how should we interpret "that he may be revealed in his time" in 2 Thessalonians 2:6b? It seems that the man of lawlessness cannot be revealed until Satan is unrestrained in heaven and then thrown to earth during the heavenly battle in Revelation 12:7–12. That is, Satan will reveal himself between event 4 and event 6. This day of the Lord is when Jesus will counterattack during the Jerusalem campaign, which seems likely to be the same day Satan will empower the man of lawlessness. The theophany on a day that will be neither day nor night and will bring thunder and an earthquake that will form a valley, as well as other events shown in figure 19, helps to tie the events of Isaiah 22, Ezekiel 38, and Zechariah 14 together to support a possible one-day event. The thunder would likely imply dark clouds.

If true, then 2 Thessalonians 2:6b can then be interpreted as follows:

> And you know what is restraining him now [the archangel Michael restraining Satan in heaven] so that he [the man of lawlessness] may be revealed in his time [as the empowered man of lawlessness on Day 1].

When Satan is thrown to earth, "and for half of the week he shall put an end to sacrifice and offering. And on the wing of abominations shall come one who makes desolate" (Dan. 9:27b; cf. Matt. 24:15). Revelation 12:7–17 has Satan being thrown to earth on Day 1, which is probably the day when the man of lawlessness is empowered. These man of lawlessness actions, whether empowered by Satan or not, would clearly reveal him (2 Thess. 2:2–4).

Chapter 5 provided evidence that the little horn would likely give up his Grecian kingdom during the first opened seal, thereby hiding his eschatological identity as the man of lawlessness until later.

---

2   See also figures 19 and 22.

According to 2 Thessalonians 2:3, the man of lawlessness will be revealed before the day of the Lord. That day seems to mean the first eschatological day of the Lord.

> Let no one deceive you in any way. For *that day* [the first eschatological day of the Lord] will not come, unless the rebellion comes first, and the man of lawlessness is revealed, the son of destruction. (2 Thess. 2:3, emphasis added)

Finally, as previously discussed, event 4 (Satan thrown to earth followed by the Antichrist in the temple and then persecution) must occur prior to event 6 (the first eschatological day of the Lord). The man of lawlessness would clearly be identified as described in figure 22 when he is empowered by Satan. Those who are wise will be able to identify the man of lawlessness much earlier in Revelation 13:18 with the correct 666 interpretation method.

FIGURE 22: MAN OF LAWLESSNESS REVEALED

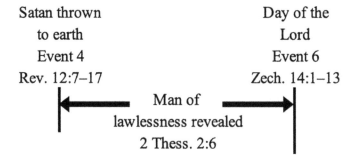

CONCLUSION

The Jerusalem campaign on the first eschatological day of the Lord will likely begin on the same day, after Gog invades Israel on Day 1. Since the wide valley forming east of Jerusalem is expected to make international news, it is possible that those in the world may be able to see Jesus, the two witnesses, the false prophet, and the man of lawlessness (whether empowered or not).

The revealing of the man of lawlessness appears to occur on Day 1.

Chapter 8

Beyond Day 1: Eschatological Day of the Lord and Day of Christ

PURPOSE

This chapter will examine six eschatological days of the Lord and three days of Christ beyond the first day of the Lord discussed in the previous chapter. These two chapters are not intended to necessarily provide a complete list of all the eschatological days of the Lord, only enough to prove the point that the day of the Lord is not a general event, though composed of seven likely unique events. The day of the Lord and the day of Christ have confused many. All the various day of the Lord events in this chapter are associated with judgment. But the day of Christ is associated wholly with reward and blessing through His coming. The first and second great eschatological theophanies are for the elect (the church) and Israel, and should be considered the day of Christ. The third great eschatological theophany will be shown to have both a judgment and blessing component.

SEVENTH OPENED SEAL: THE FIRST DAY OF CHRIST

As discussed in chapter 3, the first eschatological day of Christ is the first resurrection and rapture. This event will occur at the end of the seventh opened seal in Revelation 8:5. This great eschatological theophany is the same theophany with "peals of thunder, rumblings, flashes of lightning, and an earthquake" as later described in Revelation 11:19 and 16:18. The day of Christ is associated with Titus 2:13: "waiting for our blessed hope, the appearing of the glory of our great God and Savior Jesus Christ." Why does Titus 2:13 refer to this as the blessed hope? It is the rapture of those who have been spiritually saved and just lived through the great tribulation: "Then we who are alive, who are left, will be caught up together with them in the clouds to meet the Lord in the air, and so we will always be with the Lord" (1 Thess. 4:17). The first eschatological day of Christ occurs prior to and on the same day as the third eschatological day of the Lord.

You wait for the revealing of our *Lord Jesus Christ*, who will sustain you to the end, guiltless in the day of our *Lord Jesus Christ*. (1 Cor. 1:7–8, emphasis added)

On the *day of our Lord Jesus* you will boast of us as we will boast of you. (2 Cor. 1:14, emphasis added)

I am sure of this, that he who began a good work in you will bring it to completion at the day of *Jesus Christ* … so that you may approve what is excellent, and so be pure and blameless for the *day of Christ*. (Phil. 1:6, 10, emphasis added)

[Hold] fast to the word of life, so that in the *day of Christ* I may be proud that I did not run in vain or labor in vain. (Phil. 2:16, emphasis added)

SIXTH OPENED SEAL: THE SECOND ESCHATOLOGICAL DAY OF THE LORD

The second day of the Lord is when the wrath of the Lord begins in the sixth opened seal. Death could occur from tsunamis for those living near coast caused by the great earthquake of Revelation 6:12. Though otherwise the day of Lord is considered to be the after effects of the wicked hiding in the rocks, throwing away their idols after expecting massive destruction. Instead of death, they will be brought low and humbled later, which is likely during the seventh opened seal of normal light. (Isa. 2:12, 18–19).

FIRST BLOWN TRUMPET: THE THIRD ESCHATOLOGICAL DAY OF THE LORD

The third eschatological Day of the Lord begins with the first blown trumpet of the wrath of God, though just after and on the same day as the resurrection and rapture. "While people are saying, 'There is peace and security,' then sudden destruction [the wrath of God with the first blown trumpet] will come upon them as labor pains come upon a pregnant woman, and they will not escape" (1 Thess. 5:3). But verse 4 applies to a different group, who are believers: "But you are not in darkness, brothers, for that day to surprise you like a thief." So those who are spiritually saved would expect the rapture of the first eschatology theophany just before the third day of the Lord in Revelation 8:6ff. Those who are not believers would not expect it.

FIGURE 23: THE FIRST ESCHATOLOGICAL DAY OF CHRIST AND THIRD DAY OF THE LORD

Genesis	Matthew	Luke	1 Thessalonians	Revelation
	Like a thief in the night (24:43)		"The day of the Lord will come life a thief" (5:2)	
"For in seven days" (7:4a)		Planting and building as in the days of Lot (daylight) (17:26–27)		Opened seal 7: Silence in heaven for 7.5 days (8:1–4)
		Lightning flashes (17:24)		Peals of thunder rumblings, flashes of lightning (8:5)
		Rapture and wrath on same day (17:27–30)		Rapture and trumpet wrath (7; 8:5–7)

FIFTH BLOWN TRUMPET: THE FOURTH ESCHATOLOGICAL DAY OF THE LORD

The fifth blown trumpet has apocalyptic images coming from the furnace of the bottomless pit, which is Hades (Joel 2:1–11; Rev. 9:1–11). These images represent the apocalyptic horror that will last 150 days. Imagine agony and horror that is so bad that people will seek death but not be able to find it. Figure 24 shows common themes between Joel 2, Amos 5, and Revelation 8 and 9.

FIGURE 24: THE FOURTH ESCHATOLOGICAL DAY OF THE LORD AND FIFTH BLOWN TRUMPET

Joel 2	Amos 5	Revelation 8, 9
Trumpet blown (v. 1)		Fifth angel's trumpet blown (9:1)
Day of darkness (v. 2)	Darkness (vv. 18, 20)	The sun darkened (9:2)
Fire before and after (v. 3)		Fire before and after (8:10; 9:18)
Appearance of horses (v. 4)		Locusts appear like horses (9:7)
Greatness of the day of the Lord (v. 11)	Day of the Lord like a man fleeing a lion to meet a bear or being bitten by a snake (vv. 18–19)	Allowed to torment but not kill (9:5)

SECOND ROW: DARKNESS

One of the most important common themes among these Scriptures is the image of darkness. During the seventieth week of Daniel and the thirty days of the poured bowls, only five events involve darkness, as discussed in chapter 4 and later in this chapter. Since there are a total of twenty-one events (seven opened seals, seven blown trumpets, and seven poured bowls) with only five involving darkness, this helps to greatly narrow down the placement of eschatological Scripture.

THIRD ROW: FIRE BEFORE AND AFTER

Another common theme among these Scriptures is that "fire devours before them, and behind them a flame burns" (Joel 2:3a). The fire *before* can be found when the third trumpet sounds: "The third angel blew his trumpet, and a great star fell from heaven, blazing like a torch" (Rev. 8:10a). The fire *after* can be found when the sixth blown trumpet sounds: "By these three plagues a third of mankind was killed, by the fire" (Rev. 9:18a). These

Scriptures by themselves help identify the third eschatological day of the Lord to be either at the fourth or fifth blown trumpet.

JEWISH EXILE ENDS AND SPIRITUAL SALVATION

About the time Jacob's trouble ends, the Jewish remnant will make their way back to Jerusalem (Isa. 11:11–12; 27:12–13; Hos. 11:10–11). After or perhaps during this exile, the remnant will be spiritually saved (Isa. 1:27; Zech. 12:9–12; Rom. 11:11, 25–27). This is when "the sun shall be turned to darkness, and the moon to blood, before the great and awesome day of the LORD comes. And it shall come to pass that everyone who calls on the name of the LORD shall be saved" (Joel 2:31–32a). Being saved "before the great and awesome day of the LORD" seems to indicate that they will be saved before the Jehoshaphat campaign. Other Scriptures associating the remnant of Israel being spiritually saved are Isaiah 10:20–21, Ezekiel 39:29, Zechariah 12:9–12, and Romans 9:27. Jacob's trouble is the time when those remaining Jews will be brought through fire to be refined until they call on the Lord's name. Then the Lord will say "'They are my people'; and they will say, 'The LORD is my God'" (Zech. 13:9c).

> And on that day [the Jehoshaphat campaign] I will seek to destroy all the nations that come against Jerusalem. And I will pour out on the house of David and the inhabitants of Jerusalem a spirit of grace and pleas for mercy, so that, when they look on me, on him whom they have pierced, they shall mourn for him, as one mourns for an only child, and weep bitterly over him, as one weeps over a firstborn. On that day the mourning in Jerusalem will be as great as the mourning for Hadad-rimmon in the plain of Megiddo. (Zech. 12:9–11)

> In that day the remnant of Israel and the survivors of the house of Jacob will no more lean on him who struck them, but will lean on the LORD, the Holy One of Israel, in truth. A remnant will return, the remnant of Jacob [Israel], to the mighty God. (Isa. 10:20–21)

> And Isaiah cries out concerning Israel: "Though the number of the sons of Israel be as the sand of the sea, only a remnant of them will be saved." (Rom. 9:27)

Lest you be wise in your own sight, I do not want you to be unaware of this mystery, brothers: a partial hardening has come upon Israel, until the fullness of the Gentiles has come in. And in this way *all Israel will be saved*, as it is written, "The Deliverer will come from Zion, he will banish ungodliness from Jacob." (Rom. 11:25–26, emphasis added)

SIXTH BLOWN TRUMPET: THE FOURTH DAY OF THE LORD AND THE JEHOSHAPHAT CAMPAIGN

The Jehoshaphat campaign is the second of Jesus's three eschatological military campaigns. Joel 3:2 identifies the location of this battle as the Valley of Jehoshaphat. As shown in chapter 2, the Jehoshaphat campaign is the only eschatological event of darkness, blood, and fire. These three destructive wrath of God events can be found below, as well in Zephaniah 1:14–18 and Isaiah 13:6–13.

In figure 25 below, the second row's common theme is the battle occurring during the sixth blown trumpet of God's wrath (Joel 2:15; Rev. 9:13; 11:15). The bridegroom leaving his room in Joel 2:16 is a metaphor that the marriage supper of the Lord to come in Revelation 19:6–8 is not far away. The bridegroom is Jesus, as He told us in Mark 2:19.

The fifth row's common theme is darkness. In Joel 2:31 the sun is darkened before the day of the Lord, and in Revelation 14:17–19, there is no reference to clouds. Though there are clouds in Revelation 14:14–16, which represent daylight, Revelation 14:17 is considered to be a separate day from Revelation 14:18–19. Else, why would the angel of Revelation 14:17, who came out of the temple, not wait a few moments for the next angel in Revelation 14:18? Therefore, it appears there are two days of darkness. The day of Revelation 14:17 is when this author believes Israel will be spiritually saved. "The sun shall be turned to darkness, and the moon to blood, before the great and awesome day of the LORD comes. And it shall come to pass that everyone who calls on the name of the LORD shall be saved" (Joel 2:31–32a). The next day of darkness is when the Jehoshaphat campaign occurs in Revelation 14:18–19, which is considered parallel with Revelation 9:13–19 and similarities to Ezekiel 39:1–24. The one-day Jehoshaphat campaign is only part of the events during the sixth blown trumpet.

FIGURE 25: JEHOSHAPHAT CAMPAIGN

Isaiah and Joel	Revelation 9	Revelation 11; 14:14–20	Malachi 4
The Valley of Jehoshaphat (Joel 3:2)			
Trumpet blown; Bridegroom leaves his room (Joel 2:15–16)	Blown trumpet 6 (v. 13)	Prior to start of blown trumpet 7 (11:15)	
	Four angels (v. 14)	Four angels (14:14–15, 17–18)	
Sickle; winepress overflowing because evil is great (Joel 3:13)		Sharp sickle; winepress of the wrath of God (14:17, 19)	
Sun darkened before the day of the Lord (Joel 2:31)		No reference to clouds (darkness) (14:17–19)	
Day of the Lord (Joel 3:14)		Wrath of God (14:19)	"The day is coming" (v. 1)
Blood and fire; year of recompense and soil into sulfur (Isa. 34:8–9; Joel 2:30)	Fire, smoke, and sulfur (vv. 17–18)	Authority of third angel over fire (14:18)	Evildoers set ablaze (v. 1)
	One-third of mankind killed (v. 18)	Blood up to a horse's bridle (14:20)	Wicked tread down (v. 3)
	Horsemen (vv. 16–17)	Horse bridle (indicates horsemen) (14:20)	

SEVENTH BLOWN TRUMPET: SECOND THEOPHANY AND SECOND DAY OF CHRIST

Just as the first great eschatological theophany was associated with the first eschatological day of Christ, the second eschatological day of Christ appears to be associated with the second great eschatological theophany. That is, Revelation 8:5 and 11:19 both refer to the same theophany of "peals of thunder, rumblings, flashes of lightning, and an earthquake." Revelation 11:19 also has heavy hail. As discussed in chapter 3, Revelation 4:5 refers to the same theophany as Revelation 4:8, identifying the one on the throne as the Lord God Almighty, which leads to the conclusion that Revelation 8:5 describes the rapture of the elect (the church). Revelation 4:5 does not have an earthquake and is in front of the throne, which represents the event occurring in heaven and not on the earth.

In a similar way, any new believers in Christ after the seventh angel blew his trumpet would seem to be raptured in Revelation 11:19 theophany. This theophany occurs in the seventh blown trumpet, which is at the end of the seventieth week. The Israel remnant is provided for 1,260 days (in Rev. 12:15–25). Before this protection is over, it seems logical that they would be physically saved. This second group of believers seems to be the resurrected and raptured from the parallel Daniel 12:2–3: "Many of those who sleep in the dust of the earth shall awake, some to everlasting life, and some to shame and everlasting contempt. And those who are wise shall shine like the brightness of the sky above; and those who turn many to righteousness, like the stars forever and ever." The remnant of Israel will have been saved earlier by calling on the name of the Lord during the sixth blown trumpet, as described in Joel 2:28–32. During the millennium, the tribes of Israel will have a unique role to perform, such as serving as priests to the Lord (Ezek. 44–46). Though the first two groups are raptured separately (Rev. 8:5; 11:19), they are both part of the one bride of Christ. Both should be associated with the first resurrection in Revelation 20:6.

> Then the angel took the censer and filled it with fire from the altar and threw it on the earth, and there were *peals of thunder, rumblings, flashes of lightning, and an earthquake.* (Rev. 8:5, emphasis added)

> Then God's temple in heaven was opened, and the ark of his covenant was seen within his temple. There were *flashes of lightning, rumblings, peals of thunder, an earthquake*, and heavy hail. (Rev. 11:19, emphasis added)

> From the throne came *flashes of lightning, and rumblings and peals of thunder, and before the throne* were burning seven torches of fire, which are the seven spirits of God. (Rev. 4:5, emphasis added)

SEVENTH BLOWN TRUMPET: DAY 1,260 – ONE DAY EVENT?

In this section, we will compare the first eschatological day of Christ (rapture of the elect) to the second eschatological day of Christ (rapture of Israel) to determine whether an analogy can be made to a one-day rapture event on Day 1,260.

On Day 1 we see Satan thrown down to earth in Revelation 12:13. He then pursues the woman (Israel), who escapes and is then nourished for 1,260 days (three and a half years according to the counting in Daniel) in verses 6 and 14. So a remnant of Israel will be provided for until Day 1,260.

As discussed in chapter 2, the two witnesses will be on earth until the end of the sixth blown trumpet. The purpose of the two witnesses seems to be to witness to the Jews during Jacob's trouble. So when they leave earth their mission will have been completed.

The same rapture and theophany phrase during the seventh opened seal in Revelation 8:5 occurs during the seventh blown trumpet in Revelation 11:19. As we saw in chapter 3, almost all scholars accept that the (first) rapture will occur in one day as in the days of Noah and Lot.

These three points provide some support for the second theophany being a one-day event on Day 1,260. Therefore, it could be when the remnant of Israel's last day of protection is over, them and any new believers will be raptured. Some may say establishing a specific day (Day 1,260) for a rapture is not allowed in Scripture since "But concerning that day and hour no one knows, not even the angels of heaven, nor the Son, but the Father only" (Matt. 24:36). However, this Scripture from the Olivet Discourse appears to apply to only the first eschatological theophany for the Gentiles. Revelation 1:7 supports this: "Behold, he is coming with the clouds, and every eye will see him, even those who pierced him, and all tribes of the earth will wail on account of him. Even so. Amen." The tribes are Israel, who are mourning since they recognize they missed the first rapture. In the second rapture in Revelation 11:19, they are expected to be taken to Jerusalem for the béma judgment. Therefore, Revelation 1:7 does not seem to apply to the second or third rapture theophany events.

FIGURE 26: UPDATED THREE GREAT ESCHATOLOGICAL THEOPHANIES

First theophany	Second theophany	Third theophany
Opened seal 7	Blown trumpet 7	Poured bowl 7

Day 1	Day of Christ	Day 1260	Day 1290?
	Rev. 8:5; then Rev. 7	Rev. 11:19; Dan. 12:2–3	Rev. 16:18; Matt. 25:31–46

BÉMA

Strong's Concordance defines the Greek noun *béma* (pronounced bay'-ma) as "a step, raised place" and, by implication, "a tribunal."[1] In Romans 14:10, it refers to the judgment seat of Christ: "we will all stand before the judgment seat of God; for it is written, 'As I live, says the Lord, every knee shall bow to me, and every tongue shall confess to God.' So then each of us will give an account of himself to God" (Rom. 14:10b–12). Revelation 11:18b describes this same event as "the time for the dead to be judged, and for rewarding your servants, the prophets and saints," which is part of the seventh blown trumpet. This appears to occur within God's temple immediately after the second rapture. This is where both of those who are raptured (elect and Israel) separately, now represent the one bride, will stand before Christ individually to be judged. All those standing before Christ will have already been spiritually saved on earth. "For we must all appear before the judgment seat of Christ, so that each one may receive what is

---

1   James Strong, *Strong's Exhaustive Concordance of the Bible*, Bible Hub, s.v. "968 *béma*," accessed April 8, 2021, https://biblehub.com/greek /968.htm.

due for what he has done in the body, whether good or evil" (2 Cor. 5:10). This judgment is not for condemnation but for us to give an accounting of our lives on earth. Examples of being faithful include witnessing (Matt. 28:18–20), using your spiritual gifts (1 Cor. 12:1–11), and being victorious over sin (Rom. 6:1–4).

> According to the grace of God given to me, like a skilled master builder I laid a foundation, and someone else is building upon it. Let each one take care how he builds upon it. For no one can lay a foundation other than that which is laid, which is Jesus Christ. Now if anyone builds on the foundation with gold, silver, precious stones, wood, hay, straw—each one's work will become manifest, for the Day will disclose it, because it will be revealed by fire, and the fire will test what sort of work each one has done. If the work that anyone has built on the foundation survives, he will receive a reward. If anyone's work is burned up, he will suffer loss, though he himself will be saved, but only as through fire. (1 Cor. 3:10–15)

WHERE IS ISRAEL RAPTURED IN REVELATION 11:19?

As discussed in chapter 8, Israel is raptured at the end of the second septet of Revelation 11:19, though where are they taken to? Let's consider the second multitude rejoicing in heaven is eight chapters later, in Revelation 19:1–5. This large of a chapter gap makes it basically impossible to interpret these chapters as being the same chronologically. Basically, Israel does not appear able to be raptured to heaven in Revelation 11:19.

If Israel is not raptured to heaven in Revelation 11:19, then where are they raptured to? As discussed in chapter 1, we know scripturally that being raptured does not necessarily mean going to heaven. Consider Phillip, who was raptured (in Acts 8:39) horizontally, away from the Ethiopian eunuch to the town of Azotus. There is a strong possibility that Israel may also be raptured somewhat horizontally to the béma judgment location of Revelation 11:15–18. This location is where God Almighty starts to reign with the béma judgment.

Scripture supports Jesus's reigning on earth in the midst of Jerusalem (Zech. 8:3; 20–24; Jer. 23:5; Luke 1:32–33) and not in heaven. Revelation 11:17 says "You have taken your great power and begun to reign."

SIXTH BOWL POURED: ARMAGEDDON CAMPAIGN

The Armageddon campaign is the last of Jesus's three eschatological military campaigns represented as the sixth day of the Lord. It occurs when the sixth bowl is poured out (Rev. 16:12–16; cf. 19:11–21). This campaign is on the "great day of God the Almighty" (Rev. 16:14b), which is considered the sixth eschatological day of the Lord. The one bride of Christ (the elect and Israel) will have earlier attended the marriage supper of the Lamb. During the marriage supper, they will clothe themselves in "fine linen, bright and pure" (Rev. 19:8b). So they could be part of the Armageddon campaign since those in battle are clothed in the same clothing: "And the armies of heaven, arrayed in fine linen, white and pure, were following him on white horses" (Rev. 19:14).

SEVENTH BOWL POURED: THE THIRD GREAT ESCHATOLOGICAL THEOPHANY

The third great eschatological theophany, seventh day of the Lord, is during the seventh poured bowl in Revelation 16:18. This theophany has the same theophany phrase as in Revelation 8:5 and 11:19. However, this third theophany appears different from the other two. First, the *béma* judgment in Jerusalem has already occurred in Revelation 11:18. Second, the marriage supper has also already occurred in Revelation 19:6–10. Third, the sheep and goats are the only group not discussed in Scripture as being spiritually saved. They will be judged according to six acts of mercy to Jews since they seem to not have come to spiritual salvation. The sheep and goat judgment will occur when Jesus sits on his throne (Matt. 25:31).

SEVENTH BOWL: SIX ACTS OF MERCY TO THE JEWS

The Son of Man will separate the sheep and goats when he sits on his glorious throne (Matt. 25:31). This is their judgment, which has a different set of criteria than the first two great eschatological theophanies. The King's criteria is based on six acts of mercy they showed to "my brothers," as Jesus described in Matthew 25:31–36. Since Jesus is Jewish, this means showing mercy to the Jews. These acts of mercy seem to have occurred during Jacob's trouble, when many Jews were foreigners in exile or else generally in persecution. The sheep are the righteous, and the goats are the wicked. The six acts of mercy are listed below. The parable of the lost sheep (Matt. 18:12–14; Luke 15:3–7) can be associated with this rapture group who will escape death. This is analogous to the shepherd (Jesus) leaving the ninety-nine to look for the one lost sheep. The separation of the sheep and goats is expected to occur sometime during the period from Day 1,290 (the seventh poured bowl in Rev. 16:18) to as late as the first day of the millennium (Dan. 12:12). As discussed in chapter 11, the sheep are expected to be reigned over in the millennial, live long lives, though eventually die. Therefore, their rapture in Revelation 16:18 would not be to heaven, though somewhat horizontally. The location would likely be Jerusalem for the sheep (righteous) and goats (wicked) to be separated.

1) "I was hungry and you gave me food" (Matt. 25:35).

2) "I was thirsty and you gave me drink" (Matt. 25:35; cf. Mark 9:41).

3) "I was a stranger and you welcomed me" (Matt. 25:35).

4) "I was naked and you clothed me" (Matt. 25:36).

5) "I was sick and you visited me" (Matt. 25:36).

6) "I was in prison and you came to me" (Matt. 25:36).

These sheep are likely to attend the marriage supper as described in Matthew 22:1–10 and Revelation 19:6–10. The sheep appear to be analogous to those last few who are searched for in the main roads in verse 7: "Go therefore to the main roads and invite to the wedding feast as many as you find" (Matt. 22:9). The other analogy is to the one lost sheep of one hundred (in Matt. 18:12–14 and Luke 16:3–7).

Those in Matthew 22:11-13 without a wedding garment are likely the goats (wicked) who had no mercy acts to the Jews. They are thrown out into the darkness.

SEVENTH BOWL: RAPTURE AND RESURRECTION TO HEAVEN

It was argued earlier that Israel is raptured horizontally in second great theophany of Revelation 11:19 to Jerusalem to attend the béma judgment with the elect. Consider when the elect was raptured earlier in Revelation 8:5 they were taken to heaven in Revelation 7:9–17. For the elect to also attend the béma they must leave heaven to get to Jerusalem. After the theophany for Israel, when they meet Jesus in the sky, they will also have eternal bodies.

After the béma for the bride of Christ (the elect and Israel) they will participate with Jesus in the marriage supper, and then rejoicing in heaven, before likely participating in the battle of Armageddon. During the marriage supper the bride's white robes (Rev. 7:9) would be exchanged for fine linen (Rev. 19:8). This new understanding points to when the third great theophany of Revelation 16:18 occurs it will include only the sheep and goats to be separated. The sheep and goat judgment will occur when Jesus sits on his throne (Matt. 25:31).

The goats (wicked) will be judged to eternal fire (Matt. 25:41). The sheep (righteous) will be judged according to the six acts of mercy, the sheep likely become the subjects being reigned over and having children during the millennium.

SEVENTH BOWL: ONE DAY EVENT ON DAY 1,290?

The seventh angel pours out his bowl of God's wrath in Revelation 16:17. This is the last poured bowl. The next verse is the third theophany. These two back-to-back Scriptures give a strong impression that the seventh poured bowl could be a one-day event, just as Revelation 8:5 and 11:19 are thought to be. If so, then the third theophany could possibly occur on Day 1,290.

CONCLUSION

There appear to be seven separate future eschatological days of the Lord, which forms a septet. These days of the Lord demonstrate that the seven durations of time cannot always be interpreted as one day. For example, the fourth day of the Lord for the fifth blown trumpet is 150 days long in Revelation 9:1–11. These examples show that the day of the Lord is associated with judgment. The day of Christ is associated with the blessed hope: "waiting for our blessed hope, the appearing of the glory of our great God and Savior Jesus Christ" (Titus 2:13). This author considers the second theophany to be a second eschatological day of Christ occurring on Day 1,260.

There are two great multitudes who arrive in heaven. The first, in Revelation 7:9–17, are the elect who come from the first great eschatological theophany. The second multitude, in Revelation 19:1–5, appear to be the bride of Christ (elect and Israel) coming from the béma judgment in Jerusalem. The bride (Church and Israel) will stand before the judgment seat of Christ to be judged. This is not for condemnation but for reward since all have been spiritually saved while on earth. The one bride of Christ will attend the marriage supper of Revelation 19:6–10.

The third great eschatological theophany appears to be when the sheep and goats are taken on about Day 1,290 (end of the third septet of Rev. 16:18). They will be separated according to whether they showed any of the six acts of mercy to Jews. according to Jesus's criteria in Matthew 25:31–46.

Figure 27 provides an overview of these eschatological days of the Lord and of Christ. After the third theophany, the sheep will be determined to be righteous, and the goats will be determined to be wicked. Therefore, the event is labeled as the day of the Lord (judgment) for the goats and the day of Christ (blessing) for the sheep.

Figure 28 provides an overview of the three Jesus campaigns and who will return with him. Since the Jerusalem campaign is likely on Day 1, the saints will not have been raptured until later at the end of the first septet. Only the holy ones will return with him (Zech. 14:5).

During the Jehoshaphat campaign Jesus will "trodden the winepress alone and from the peoples no one was with me" (Isa. 63:3a). Isaiah 63:1 has Jesus returning "from Edom in crimsoned garments from Bozrah." where he rescued the Israel remnant.

During the third campaign Jesus will return with the armies of heaven. The army appears to include those who attended the marriage supper of the Lamb since they are clothed in white linen in both Revelation 19:8, 14.

FIGURE 27: ESCHATOLOGICAL DAYS OF THE LORD AND OF CHRIST OVERVIEW

Eschatological Events	Description	Starts	Length	Judgment/ Blessing
First day of the Lord	Jerusalem campaign	Day 1	1 day?	Judgment
Second day of the Lord	Wrath of the Lamb	Opened sixth and seventh seals	34–40 days	Judgment (wicked brought low)
First day of Christ	First theophany: Resurrection and rapture	Last day of opened seal 7	Less than 24 hours	Blessing (rapture)
Third day of the Lord	Start of the wrath of God	Blown trumpet 1	Unknown	Judgment
Fourth day of the Lord	People seek death but do not find it	Blown trumpet 5	150 days	Judgment
Fifth day of the Lord	Jehoshaphat campaign	Blown trumpet 6	1 day?	Judgment
Second day of Christ	Second theophany	Blown trumpet 7	Less than 24 hours?	Blessing (rapture)
Great day of God Almighty	Armageddon campaign	Poured bowl 6	Unknown	Judgment
Day of Christ and the Lord	Third theophany: Sheep and goats	Poured bowl 7	Less than 24 hours?	Blessing (rapture) and judgment

FIGURE 28: JESUS'S ESCHATOLOGICAL WARFARE CAMPAIGNS

Eschatological Campaigns	Descriptions	Jesus alone?
First: Jerusalem	Opened seal 5, Day 1 (Zech. 14:2, 5)	No. Jesus and all the holy ones.
Second: Jehoshaphat	Blown trumpet 6 (Joel 3:2; Rev. 9:13–20)	Yes.
Third: Armageddon	Poured bowl 6 (Rev. 19:11–16)	No. Armies of heaven with Jesus.

Chapter 9

The Eighth Head and the Multiple Kingdom Coalition

PURPOSE

Current scholarly interpretation vary as to which empire the revived fourth great beast (eighth head) is from. Most say from the Roman Empire and a few from the Islamic Caliphate. This book presents a different perspective: the eighth head may be composed of multiple kingdoms.

ORIGIN OF THE MAN OF LAWLESSNESS?

In this section, we will examine the geographical origin of the man of lawlessness. "And the goat is the king of Greece. And the great horn between his eyes is the first king" (Dan. 8:21). Other verses in Daniel 8 point to the little horn coming from this kingdom. In chapter 5 we saw that the little horn will give up his kingdom and then become the man of lawlessness. On Day 1 the man of lawlessness will become empowered by Satan to become the Antichrist. This chronological sequence of events leads us to say the man of lawlessness may geographically come from the Grecian empire.

Some authors point to the beast coming from the Roman Empire since they led the assault on Jerusalem in AD 70. The destruction of the second temple, leaving no stone on top of the another, was clearly a near-prophecy fulfillment of the Olivet Discourse (Matt. 24:2). However, in the Olivet Discourse, Jesus does not explicitly say the kingdom(s) who desecrates the second temple will be exactly the same as those who desecrate the future eschatological third temple. Though this alternate geographical country analysis of the man of lawlessness could have merit.

According to Daniel 7:24 and Revelation 17:12, the ten horns are ten kings. In Revelation 13:1, the beast of the sea has ten horns. As shown in chapter 5, the ten horns (kings) are only part of a revived fourth kingdom. We also identified one of the horns as coming from the Grecian Empire. Since three of the Grecian kings were removed in Daniel (7:8, 20, 24; 8:9, 23), it is doubtful that any of the other nine kings are from the Grecian Empire.

Therefore, the country-kingdom the little horn may have control of the historical Grecian empire. It does not seem to be Europe since the Grecian empire never extended that far. Also, the Grecian empire never extended into present day Russia. As to the origin of birth of the man Scripture seems to be silent.

FIRST AND SECOND HEADS

The first two heads of Revelation 17:9–10 are the Egyptian and Assyrian Empires. The first represents Israel's slavery under Pharoah in Exodus 1–11. The second head represents the captivity of the ten northern tribes in 2 Kings 17. Daniel 2 and 7 have no reference to the first or second head.

THIRD TO FIFTH HEADS

The third head represents the Babylonian Empire of Daniel 2:37–38 and 7:4 and 17. The fourth head represents the Medo-Persian Empire of Daniel 2:39 and 7:5 and 17. The fifth head is the Grecian Empire of Daniel 2:39 and 7:6 and 17.

SIXTH HEAD: JEWISH AND ROMAN EMPIRES

The sixth head seems to be composed of two empires: Jewish and Roman.

The Jewish empire is the son of destruction and other Jews. Several decades after Jesus was crucified, the apostle John wrote about the beast who "was and is not" in Revelation 17:8. This author considers this beast to be the first son of destruction, Judas Iscariot (John 17:12b) who was Jewish. During the Passover meal "when he [Jesus] had dipped the morsel, he gave it to Judas, the son of Simon Iscariot. Then after he had taken the morsel, Satan entered into him" (John 13:26b–27a). Later that night Judas identified Jesus to the chief priests by a kiss so He would be seized (Matt. 26:47–50). There were other Jews responsible for Jesus's death, such as the crowd: "Pilate said to them, 'Then what shall I do with Jesus who is called Christ?' They all said, 'Let him be crucified'" (Matt. 27:22). Considering that day was the Passover, many in the crowd would be Jews.

The second empire of the sixth head is the Romans, who crucified Jesus under Pontius Pilate, the Roman governor who sentenced Jesus: "Then he

[Pilate] released for them Barabbas, and having scourged Jesus, delivered him to be crucified" (Matt. 27:26).

These Scriptures point to the sixth head being two entities, one being the Jewish community, including Judas Iscariot (the son of destruction), and the second being the Roman empire that crucified Jesus. The mention of the second son of destruction in 2 Thessalonians 2:3–4 has eschatological implications and refers to the man of lawlessness.

SEVENTH HEAD

Daniel 7:17 identified four great beasts as four kings. Later Daniel "desired to know the truth about the fourth beast, which was different from all the rest, exceedingly terrifying, with its teeth of iron and claws of bronze, and which devoured and broke in pieces and stamped what was left with its feet" (Dan. 7:19). Joel Richardson in his book *Mideast Beast* identified the Islamic Caliphate as being the seventh head, also known as the fourth great beast.

> The Islamic Caliphate absolutely crushed all of the Babylonian, Medo-Persian, and Greek Empires. Beyond conquering their territories, in most cases it was also successful in imposing its own culture (Arab), religion (Islam), and language (Arabic) as well.[1]

With the conquered territories, this historic fourth great beast has borders larger than the borders of the previous three great beasts combined. This fulfills the prophecy in Revelation 13:2a: "And the beast that I saw was like a leopard; its feet were like a bear's, and its mouth was like a lion's mouth." These three great beasts are the lion (first great beast) of the Babylonian Empire, the bear (second great beast) of the Medo-Persian Empire, and the leopard (third great beast) of the Grecian Empire. The Roman Empire's borders never overlapped all of the borders of these first three great beasts.[2] The Roman and Grecian Empires also never repressed other cultures and languages. This is what the Apostle Paul discovered on his second missionary journey to Greece, when he visited Mars Hill.

---

1   Joel Richardson, *Mideast Beast: The Scriptural Case for an Islamic Antichrist* (Washington, D.C.: WND Books, 2012), 77.
2   Ibid., 76-77.

> So Paul, standing in the midst of the Areopagus, said: "Men of Athens, I perceive that in every way you are very religious. For as I passed along and observed the objects of your worship, I found also an altar with this inscription: 'To the unknown god.' What therefore you worship as unknown, this I proclaim to you." (Acts 17:22–23)

Though this was in Greece, it was during the Roman Empire. The Roman Empire, as well as the previous Grecian Empire, did not want to offend any god, so they allowed for the worship of an unknown god. They did not have the repression that the Islamic Caliphate had. There was persecution of Christians during the reign of some Roman emperors, though it was for a relatively short amount of time. Therefore, the Islamic Caliphate seems to be more representative of the fourth great beast (seventh head). In 1924, the first President of the Turkish Republic, Mustafa Kemal Atatürk constitutionally abolished the institution of the caliphate.[3] "One of its heads seemed to have a mortal wound, but its mortal wound was healed, and the whole earth marveled as they followed the beast" (Rev. 13:3). The reemergence of the Islamic Caliphate about a hundred years later, as the eighth head, would seem to fulfill prophecy.

EIGHTH HEAD: MULTIPLE EMPIRE SOLUTION NEEDED

This one-empire solution for the eighth head has several eschatological problems, which seems to direct us to a multiple empire solution for the revived Grecian Empire (little horn originally) or Roman Empire (70 AD General Titus), Islamic Caliphate (nine horns), under the authority of the Antichrist (man of lawlessness and Satan).

A second alternative to the Grecian Empire is the general Titus of the historic Roman Empire could represent the coming prince the Antichrist. First, in AD 70, Jerusalem was attacked by the Roman Empire with their legions and a significant help of auxiliaries. The second temple was destroyed. According to Josephus in *The War of the Jews*, "it was so thoroughly laid even with the ground by those that dug it up to the foundation, that there was

---

3 Wikipedia, s.v. "Caliphate," accessed March 11, 2022, https://en.wikipedia.org/wiki/Caliphate.

left nothing…"[4] This fulfilled Jesus's prophesy that "there will not be left here one stone upon another that will not be thrown down" (Matt. 24:2b). Though the remaining Olivet prophecy of Matthew 24–25 has not yet been fulfilled. The reason no stone was left on another was to retrieve the gold in the temple that had melted, its heavier density causing it to slide between the stones. From the Roman historian Cornelius Tacitus in *The Histories* we see the following perspective of the battle force:

> By his courtesy and affability he called forth a willing obedience, and he often mixed with the common soldiers, while working or marching, without impairing his dignity as general. He found in Judaea three legions, the 5th, the 10th, and the 15th, all old troops of Vespasian's. To these he added the 12th from Syria, and some men belonging to the 18th and 3rd, whom he had withdrawn from Alexandria. This force was accompanied by twenty cohorts of allied troops and eight squadrons of cavalry, by the two kings Agrippa and Sohemus, by the auxiliary forces of king Antiochus, by a strong contingent of Arabs, who hated the Jews with the usual hatred of neighbours, and, lastly, by many *persons* brought from the capital and from Italy by private hopes of securing the yet unengaged affections of the *prince*.[5] (emphasis added)

We know the following from Josephus's *The War of the Jews*:

> There were also a considerable number of auxiliaries got together that came from the kings Antiochus, and Agrippa, and Sohemus, each of them contributing one thousand footmen that were archers and a thousand horsemen. *Malchus also, the king* [of] *Arabia*, sent a thousand horsemen, besides five thousand footmen, the greatest part of whom were archers; so that the whole army, including the auxiliaries sent by the kings, as well horsemen as footmen, when all were united together, amounted to *sixty thousand*.[6]

---

4   Flavius Josephus, *The War of the Jews*, in *Josephus: The Complete Works*, trans. William Whiston (Nashville: Thomas Nelson, 1998), 7.1.1.

5   Cornelius Tacitus, *The Histories*, in *The Complete Works of Tacitus* (n.p.: Digireads.com Publishing, 2013), Book 5.

6   Josephus, *War of the Jews*, 3.4.2.

Tacitus notes that there were many Roman "people" wanting to secure military recognition in the Roman Empire by someone they called the "prince." The Roman prince of AD 70 is the Roman general Titus. The association of these people and the prince seems to reflect the unfulfilled far prophecy in Daniel 9:26, where the ten kings (people) give their authority to the Antichrist (prince). We also see that the vast majority of the fighting force is not Roman. There were no more than 5,000 Western soldiers, and the remaining 55,000 to 56,000 were all Easterners.[7] According to Josephus, the total army numbered about sixty thousand, many of whom were from an auxiliary force led by King Antiochus that had a strong contingent of Arabs. This army in AD 70 may be analogous to the future ten kings having the vast majority of the military force.

Another reason for a multiple empire solution is in Daniel 7:24: "As for the ten horns, out of this kingdom ten kings shall arise, and another shall arise, after them; he shall be different from the former ones, and shall put down three kings." Daniel 8:9, this different one is identified as the little horn who will give away his goat kingdom as the man of lawlessness and then on Day 1 be empowered by Satan to become the Antichrist. Separate from the Antichrist are the ten kings. "And the ten horns that you saw are ten kings who have not yet received royal power, but they are to receive authority as kings for one hour, together with the beast" (Rev. 17:12). Considering the Antichrist will only have authority for a limited amount of time, why would he take authority away from his ten allies after only one hour of combat? The answer is "they will mix with one another in marriage, but they will not hold together, just as iron does not mix with clay" (Dan. 2:43). After the ten kings lose authority, then "these are of one mind, and they hand over their power and authority to the beast. They will make war on the Lamb, and the Lamb will conquer them, for he is Lord of lords and King of kings, and those with him are called and chosen and faithful" (Rev. 17:13–14). The ten kings giving their power and authority to the beast represents the Antichrist becoming the prince.

According to Daniel 9:26b, "the people of the prince who is to come shall destroy the city and the sanctuary." Two different entities (the people and the prince) will destroy the city and the sanctuary. They appear as a military coalition, and the prince would be the leader of the military force,

---

7   Richardson, *Mideast Beast*, 96.

who most scholars associate with the Antichrist or Gog. The people seem to be the military force who would cause the destruction.

Having multiple historic empires as the revived fourth kingdom represents a large boundary About twenty percent of the world's current population lives within the historic boundaries of the Grecian empire and the Islamic Caliphate. Their territory will likely expand when the second seal is opened, helping to fulfill the prophecy of the fourth opened seal: "And they were given authority over a fourth of the earth, to kill with sword and with famine and with pestilence and by wild beasts of the earth" (Rev. 6:8).

In Ephesians 2:1–2, Satan is described as the prince of power: "And you were dead in the trespasses and sins in which you once walked, following the course of this world, following the prince of the power of the air, the spirit that is now at work in the sons of disobedience." When Satan is thrown from heaven to earth on Day 1 in Revelation 12:7–9, his demon spirit will occupy the man of lawlessness. They will become the Antichrist.

TRAITS OF THE BEAST FROM THE SEA: ANTICHRIST

The Antichrist is composed of two beings who exist prior to Day 1. The first is a human described in 2 Thessalonians 2:3 as the man of lawlessness. Since this is a man, he will presumably be born on the earth. The second entity is Satan. On Day 1, when Satan, a spirit being, is thrown to earth (Rev. 12:7–9), he is expected to enter the man of lawlessness, a human being. When these two beings become one, the man becomes the Antichrist. This is similar to when the Holy Spirit, a spirit being, enters the body of a new Christian believer and the two become one.

The man of lawlessness will have the following traits, some empowered by Satan and some not:

- It will have ten horns and seven heads. On its horns there are ten diadems (Rev. 12:3; 13:1).
- Great red dragon (Rev. 12:3).
- It will rise from the sea (Rev. 13:1).
- Its heads will have blasphemous names on them (Rev. 13:1).
- It will have traits like a lion (first beast), a bear (second beast), and a leopard (third beast) (Dan. 7:4–6; Rev. 13:2a).

- The dragon (Satan) will give it power, a throne, and authority (Rev. 13:2b).

- One head will have a mortal wound (Rev. 13:3).

- People will worship the dragon (Rev. 13:4).

- It will have authority for forty-two months (Rev. 13:5).

- It will utter haughty and blasphemous words (Dan. 7:8; Rev. 13:5–6).

- It will make war against the saints and conquer them (Rev. 13:7).

- It will have authority over those who dwell on earth (Rev. 13:7–8).

- It will speak against the Most High (Dan. 7:25).

- It will persecute God's people (Dan. 7:25).

- It will change the law (Dan. 7:25).

- It will change the time (Dan. 7:25).

- His mark will be 666, which is "the number of a man." (Rev. 13:18).

- He will be a man of lawlessness, not an angel or a demon (2 Thess. 2:3).

- He will "stand" in the holy place on Day 1, when the great tribulation begins (Matt. 24:15–16, 31).

- He will prosper (Dan. 8:12).

- He will not abide by truth (Dan. 8:12).

- He will deal with the strongest of fortresses (Dan. 11:39).

The son of destruction refers to both the historic Judas Iscariot (John 17:12) and the eschatological man of lawlessness (2 Thess. 2:3–4). These two individuals both seem to reflect the prophecy in Revelation 17:11: "As for the beast that was and is not, it is an eighth but it belongs to the seven, and it goes to destruction."

The demonic spirit—Satan—who enters the man of lawlessness (a literal man born on earth) is the same spirit who entered Judas, who betrayed Jesus (Luke 22:3; John 13:27). The end of Satan and the man he possessed is eternal destruction. The man of lawlessness will be captured and thrown alive in the lake of fire (Rev. 19:20–21). Satan, the demonic spirit of the Antichrist, will be captured and thrown into the bottomless pit for a thousand years (Rev. 20:1–2). After the thousand years, he will also join the son of destruction in the lake of fire (Rev. 20:10).

Therefore, the man of lawlessness is the beast.

TRAITS OF FALSE PROPHET: THE BEAST FROM THE EARTH

The false prophet will have the following traits:

- He will rise out of the earth (Rev. 13:11).
- He will be a "beast" (Rev. 11:7; 19:20).
- He will have prophetically two horns like a lamb and speak like a dragon (Rev. 13:11).
- He will exercise all the authority of the beast from the sea in its presence and make everyone worship the beast whose mortal wound was healed (Rev. 13:12).
- He will perform great signs, including making fire come down (Rev. 13:13).
- He will deceive the world and tell them to make an image for the beast from the sea (Rev. 13:14).
- He will give breath to the image of the beast from the sea (Rev. 13:15).
- He will force everyone to get the mark of the beast in order to buy or sell (Rev. 13:16–17).

THREE DEMONIC SPIRITS

There are three demonic spirits: the dragon (Satan), the beast, and the false prophet described in Revelation 16:13. The false prophet was previously deduced to be the beast of the earth from Revelation 13:11–18. The beast from the sea in Revelation 13:1–10 was deduced to be the Antichrist with ten horns. This position is supported by most scholars. Though how does one equate the two beasts of Revelation 13 with the three demonic spirits of Revelation 16:13?

The answer appears that the Antichrist represents two parts of these three demonic spirits and not just one. One part is the man of lawlessness and the second part is Satan, who empowers him. Together they have "ten horns and seven heads, with ten diadems on their horns" (Rev. 13:1). The third part of the demonic spirit is the false prophet. Therefore, Revelation 13's two beasts (beast of the sea and beast of the earth) can now be equated to the three demonic spirits of Revelation 16:13. These three demonic spirits are: Satan who is the great red dragon, son of destruction who is the man of lawlessness, and the false prophet who is like a dragon. These three could be considered Satan's false representation of the Holy trinity: Father (Ancient of Days), Son (Jesus), and Holy Spirit.

Satan will be captured and thrown into the abyss for 1,000 years (Rev. 20:1–3). The false prophet and the beast will earlier be "thrown alive into the lake of fire" (Rev. 19:20). Therefore, through deduction, this described Revelation 19 beast seems to be a reference to the man of lawlessness being destroyed.

EIGHTH HEAD: PROPHETIC SYMBOLISM

Daniel 2:40–41 identifies the revived fourth kingdom, composed of prophetic feet and toes representing a divided kingdom. Since human feet normally have ten toes, the toes seem to represent the ten kings. Therefore, the feet must represent the Antichrist. The "claws of bronze" in Daniel 7:19 are analogous to the "toes," where there are ten claws or toes for a pair of feet. Equating claws to toes is similar to when King Nebuchadnezzar was driven from men and "his nails were like birds' claws" (Dan. 4:33). The toes are part of the feet that in Daniel 2:41 are described as feet of iron and clay. Therefore, the iron teeth in Daniel 7:19 seem to represent the man of lawlessness when he had a kingdom (little horn).

FIFTH KINGDOM: MESSIANIC EMPIRE

The last kingdom is when the seventh angel sounds the trumpet in Revelation 11:15b. There will be loud voices in heaven saying, "The kingdom of the world has become the kingdom of our Lord and of his Christ, and he shall reign forever and ever." This is when the Messianic Empire begins and lasts forever.

FIGURE 29: EIGHT HEADS (EMPIRES)

Kingdoms	Revelation 17	Empire	Daniel 2	Daniel 7
	First head	Egyptian	—	—
	Second head	Assyrian	—	—
First	Third head	Babylonian	Head of gold	Lion
Second	Fourth head	Medo-Persian	Chest and arms of silver	Bear
Third	Fifth head	Grecian	Belly and thighs of bronze	Leopard
	Sixth head	Roman	—	—
		Jewish		
Fourth	Seventh head	Islamic Caliphate	Legs of iron	—
Revived fourth	Revived seventh head	Revived Caliphate and Grecian or Roman	Toes of iron and clay	Bronze claws (ten horns)
		Antichrist	Feet of iron and clay	Iron teeth
Fifth		Messianic	The rock	Son of Man

KING DAVID'S THREE CHOICES

When King David sinned by taking a census, the Lord spoke through the prophet Gad to give him three choices of wrath as punishment. Two of the options were that God's hand would strike the nation; the third option was the nation would fall into enemy hands. King David decided to fall into God's hand, since he knew the Lord's mercy is great. During the great tribulation, we will not have a choice, though thankfully we can fall into God's hands as to when Satan's great persecution will end.

And when David arose in the morning, the word of the Lord came to the prophet Gad, David's seer, saying, "Go and say to David, 'Thus says the Lord, Three things I offer you. Choose one of them, that I may do it to you.'" So Gad came to David and told him, and said to him, "Shall three years of famine come to you in your land? Or will you flee three months before your foes while they pursue you? Or shall there be three days' pestilence in your land? Now consider, and decide what answer I shall return to him who sent me." Then David said to Gad, *"I am in great distress. Let us fall into the hand of the Lord, for his mercy is great; but let me not fall into the hand of man."* (2 Sam. 24:11–14, emphasis added)

CONCLUSION

The sixth prophetic head of Revelation 17:9–10 seems to represent the Jews and the Roman empire. Judas, who Satan entered, represents the son of destruction in John 17:12b. The Romans crucified Jesus under Pontius Pilate, the Roman governor (Matt. 27:26). Alternatively, the man of lawlessness could come from the little horn's Grecian empire.

According to Daniel 9:26b "the people of the prince who is to come shall destroy the city and the sanctuary." This verse refers to two different entities. The prince is a reference to Revelation 17:13, where the ten kings hand over their power and authority to the Antichrist. The people represent the ten kings, who do the vast majority of the destruction. The empire of the Antichrist is the beast coming out of the sea after Satan and his angels are thrown out of heaven to earth in Revelation 12:9. The ten kings and the Antichrist represent the eighth head of prophetic clay and iron trying to hold together (Dan. 2:40–43). They are unable to hold together in Revelation 17:12 and Daniel 2:40–43. "These [ten kings] are of one mind, and they hand over their power and authority to the beast [man of lawlessness]" (Rev. 17:13).

The three unclean spirits are the dragon (Satan), the beast (man of lawlessness), and the false prophet described in Revelation 16:13. This is where the dragon and the beast seem to be representative of the Antichrist. The three appear to be representative of a false trinity.

Chapter 10

Signs of the End of the Age

ISRAEL AND TEMPLE SACRIFICES

Arguably the most significant end-times event to occur in 1,900 years was the nation of Israel coming back into existence on May 14, 1948. During the prior diaspora, the Jewish people did not have a country to call their home. Another important event occurred on June 7, 1967, when Israel took control of the Temple Mount, paving the way for a future third temple to be built.

Prior to the eschatological abomination of the temple by the Antichrist, spoken of in Daniel 9:27, a third temple must be built and daily sacrifices and offerings must begin. The Bible gives no indication of how long before Day 1 the temple will be completed or when the temple sacrifices and offerings will begin. In order for sacrifices and offerings to begin, the following events must occur, many of which have been completed relatively recently.

1) *Red heifer.* For daily temple sacrifices to start again, a red heifer is needed, as prescribed in Numbers 19. The red cow must be without blemish and never have been under a yoke. The Temple Institute monitors red cows to see if they meet these and other requirements.[1] So far there has not been an unblemished red heifer found.

2) *Temple furnishings.* The Temple Institute has already built all the temple furnishings for the priests to begin the sacrifices.[2]

3) *Priests' clothing.* Priests who will perform within the future third temple are required to wear specific types of clothing, described in Exodus 28. The holy garments are for the high priest (vv. 2–39) and

---

1   The Temple Institute, "Red Heifer Update," March 1, 2021, https://templeinstitute.org/.
2   The Messianic Jewish Bible Society, "The Temple Vessels are Ready for the Rebuilding of Jerusalem's Third Temple," accessed March 18, 2021, https://free.messianicbible.com/feature/the-temple-vessels-are-ready-for -the-rebuilding-of-jerusalems-third-temple/.

for ordinary priests (vv. 40–43). In 2008 the Temple Institute was ready to begin clothing manufacturing.[3]

4) *Training.* In August 2016, the Temple Institute announced it is opening a school to train Levitical priests for their eventual service in a new temple.[4]

5) *Temple mount structure.* Historically, the temple has been either a tabernacle or a temple. A tabernacle is a large, intricately designed tent, such as the one Israel used when they wandered the desert for forty years (Ex. 26; 35:11). A temple is a permanent structure, such as the first temple built by Solomon (1 Kings 5:13–18; 9:10–11). The temple measured in Revelation 11:2 appears to be the third temple since that same verse has the two witnesses arriving then.

GOSPEL PREACHED TO THE WORLD

Prior to the return of Jesus, the Great Commission of Matthew 28:16–20 must be fulfilled. The CRU (Campus Crusade) Jesus Film Project announced that as of May 27, 2020, the "JESUS" film (classic version) has been translated into 1,838 languages and has been shown to more than 8.1 billion people, with 572 million people indicating decisions for Christ following a film showing.[5] Even if Day 1 arrives and the gospel has not quite been preached to everyone in the world, it seems the proclamation of the first angel in Revelation 14:6–7 will likely complete this prophecy.

3　Danielle Kubes, "Third Temple Preparations Begin with Priestly Garb," *Jerusalem Post*, July 1, 2008, https://www.jpost.com/Jewish-World/Jewish-News/Third-Temple-preparations-begin-with-priestly-garb.

4　"Temple Institute Announces School to Train Levitical Priests," Jewish Telegraphic Agency, August 2, 2016, https://www.jta.org/2016/08/02/israel/temple-institute-announces-school-to-train-levitical-priests.

5　"Official Jesus Film Project Ministry Statistics—May 27, 2020," Jesus Film Project, https://www.jesusfilm.org/about/learn-more/statistics.html.

Then I saw another angel flying directly overhead, with an eternal gospel to proclaim to those who dwell on earth, to every nation and tribe and language and people. And he said with a loud voice, "Fear God and give him glory, because the hour of his judgment has come, and worship him who made heaven and earth, the sea and the springs of water." (Rev. 14:6–7)

MIDDLE EAST PEACE PLAN: ABRAHAM ACCORD

On January 29, 2020 a peace plan was announced by Israeli Prime Minister Benjamin Netanyahu and the President of the United States, Donald Trump.[6] The fifty-page outline calls for a four-year freeze in new Israeli settlement construction, during which time details of a comprehensive agreement would be negotiated. If the Palestinians do not sign the treaty by the January 29, 2024 deadline, then Israel may restart building their settlements in the Palestinian West Bank and the Palestinians would lose $50 billion from the US in investment funding.

Since then, the Palestinians did not show an interest, such that Israel has continued building settlements. Though a future treaty has the potential of being the start of the seventieth week. If so, this would require a massive construction project where Israel would presumably need to allow construction equipment and foreigners on its sovereign land for a certain amount of time to build the contracted infrastructure.

KNOWING THE TIMES

Although some may still dismiss the idea that we can know the season of Jesus's return, we must remember that Jesus rebuked the Sadducees and Pharisees for not knowing the sign of Christ's first coming, though they could tell the signs of the weather (Matt. 16:1–3). We have a vast amount of Scripture about the Lord's second coming, compared with His first coming. How much more should we be observant of the season of the Lord's second coming! Considering all of these recent events in the Middle East, I would be surprised if the seventieth week of Daniel did not start by 2030.

---

6   Wikipedia, s.v. "Trump Peace Plan," accessed March 28, 2021, https://en.wikipedia.org/wiki/Trump_peace_plan.

REQUIREMENTS FOR DAY 1 TO BEGIN

All of the components needed to start the temple sacrifices are in place except for locating an unblemished red heifer and building the third temple. The impression is that they are not far away. These events must occur before the great tribulation can begin. But there are other non-temple requirements that must also be fulfilled before Day 1, including the making of a strong covenant (Dan. 9:27), the first four opened seals (Rev. 6:1–8), the revealing of the man of lawlessness and the falling away (2 Thess. 2:1–4), the preaching of the gospel to the world (likely completed by the first angel's warning in Rev. 14:6–7), and Satan being thrown to earth (Rev. 12:7–17). The ram and goat near fulfilled prophecy could also be a far prophecy to be fulfilled before the start of the seventieth week.

CONCLUSION

Jesus is returning soon. Maranatha!

Chapter 11

Millennium, Resurrection, and Beyond

TYPES OF EARTH: OLD, OLD TWISTED CRUST, AND NEW

To help understand the events into the millennium and beyond, we need to associate them with the three types of earth: the old earth, the twisted crust of the old earth, and the new earth. For simplicity, the earlier forms of earth in Genesis 1 were not included. The first earth is the one we are now living in. This author calls it the old earth to distinguish it from the other two. The second earth occurs between the chronology of the old and new earth when the old earth's crust is twisted: "Behold, the Lord will empty the earth and make it desolate, and he will twist its surface and scatter its inhabitants" (Isa. 24:1). This event is also described in Revelation 16:19–21, which occurs on the last day of the seventh poured bowl. We previously saw that this will likely occur on Day 1,290, when the old earth's twisted crust is formed. Then forty-five days later the earth will be populated again. The third earth is the new earth after the millennium. "Then I saw a new heaven and a new earth, for the first heaven and first earth had passed away, and the sea was no more" (Rev. 21:1).

The millennium is considered the seventh and last millennium on the old earth. For example, if the seventieth week of Daniel ends in 2030, then that would mean the Hebrew calendar should be the year 6000. The current Hebrew year in March 2021 is 5781. The Gregorian month and year needs to be included when equating to a Hebrew year since their year begins on Tishri 1, which is in the Gregorian month of September or October. Their calendar begins when Adam and Eve were created. Ideally, the Hebrew calendar would be the year 6000 when the new millennium starts, though Hebrew scholars recognize their calendar is short about 180 to 210 years. This author uses an upper range of 210 instead of 217 years' difference since if the seventieth week of Daniel had already started, we should have recognized it. This simple analysis shows we are nearing the return of Christ. Maranatha!

UNDERSTANDING ISAIAH 65:17–25

The ESV titles Isaiah 65:17–25 as "New Heavens and a New Earth." Isaiah 65:17 starts off with "For behold, I create new heavens and a new earth, and the former things shall not be remembered or come into mind." Isaiah 65:18 continues, "But be glad and rejoice forever in that which I create." This can seem confusing. My interpretation is that verse 17 is the new earth (after the millennium) being compared to the old earth with a twisted crust (during the millennium) in verses 18–25. Isaiah 65:18–25 must apply to the millennium for two reasons.

First, Isaiah 65:20 refers to death. Since the new earth will have no death (Rev. 21:4), these verses cannot apply to the new earth. Second, verse 23 refers to bearing children, though the description of the new earth in Revelation 21 has no such reference. Also, if children were born on the new earth then they would need to be judged to either eternal life or judgment. Revelation 21 has no such future judgment or Great White Throne event.

FIGURE 30: EARTH'S TWISTED CRUST AND THE NEW EARTH

	Old (first) earth's twisted crust	New (second) earth
When?	Millennium (Isa. 24:14–16; Rev. 20:1–5)	Post millennium (Rev. 21)
Populated by which elect?	Elect (church) who are beheaded (Rev. 20:4–5)	All of the elect (Rev. 20:1, 11–15)
Populated by others?	Third theophany (sheep) (Matt. 25:31–40; Rev. 16:18)	Great White Throne (Rev. 20:11–15)
Earth?	Old with twisted crust (Isa. 24:1; Rev. 16:20)	New earth (Isa. 65:17; Rev. 21)
Death?	Yes, after long lives (Isa. 65:20)	No (Isa. 25:8; Rev. 21:4)
Sin?	Yes, Satan released (Rev. 20:2–3)	No, Satan killed earlier (Rev. 20:7–10)
Seas?	Yes (Isa. 24:15; Ezek. 47:8–9; Zech. 14:8)	No (Rev. 21:1)
Children born?	Yes (only to sheep?) (Isa. 65:23)	No
Animal sacrifices?	Yes (Ezek. 46–47)	No

RESURRECTION

There are two types of resurrection. "Do not marvel at this, for an hour is coming when all who are in the tombs will hear his voice and come out, those who have done good to the resurrection of life, and those who have done evil to the resurrection of judgment" (John 5:28–29).

FIRST RESURRECTION TO LIFE

The first eschatological resurrection is this: "For this we declare to you by a word from the Lord, that we who are alive, who are left until the coming of the Lord, will not precede those who have fallen asleep. ... Then we who are alive, who are left, will be caught up together with them in the clouds to meet the Lord in the air, and so we will always be with the Lord" (1 Thess. 4:15, 17). Chapter 8 discusses the three great eschatological theophanies in more detail.

EARTH RESTORED AND ISRAEL BECOMES LIKE GARDEN OF EDEN

This process starts during the seventh poured bowl, when the old earth's crust is twisted in Isaiah 24:1. Revelation 16:20 describes this same event: "And every island fled away, and no mountains were to be found." The earth will be restored during the forty-five days from Day 1,291 to 1,335. At the end of these forty-five days (Day 1,335), the earth will be ready to be populated with humans. Ezekiel 36:35 describes Israel being like the garden of Eden.

POPULATING EARTH: OLD TWISTED CRUST

After the old earth is restored by twisting its crust, it can be populated again. The first population event occurs at the start of the millennium. The second population event for the new earth occurs after the millennium and the Great White Throne judgment are complete.[1] The first population event is composed of three groups.

The first group will reign with the Lord on earth as spoken of in Revelation 20:4. They will have immortal bodies.

The second group are also those who appear to be reigning on earth with Christ. This author's opinion is that this group will include those who were raptured for three reasons. First, see the Revelation 20:4 interpretation below. The use of "and" seems to separate this sentence into two different groups.

> "Also I saw the souls of those [first group] who had been beheaded for the testimony of Jesus and for the word of God, and those [second group] who had not worshiped the beast or its image and had not received its mark on their foreheads or their hands. They came to life and reigned with Christ for a thousand years." (Rev. 20:4b)

1　　See figure 31.

The second reason is found in 1 Thessalonians 4:17: "Then we who are alive, who are left, will be caught up together with them in the clouds to meet the Lord in the air, and so we will always be with the Lord." Ezekiel 43:7 says the Lord will dwell in the midst of the people of Israel forever. Since those raptured will always be with the Lord and he is reigning on earth during the millennium, it would therefore seem those raptured would be with the Lord on the earth during the millennium.

The third reason is that Jews are required to perform millennium daily sacrifices. The Jews are expected to be raptured in the second theophany. Therefore, it seems the Jews raptured during the second theophany should be on the earth during the millennium (Rev. 20:4).

> While the man was standing beside me, I heard one speaking to me out of the temple, and he said to me, "Son of man, this is the place of my throne and the place of the soles of my feet, where I will dwell in the midst of the people of Israel forever." (Ezek. 43:6–7a)

The third group seem to be the sheep who come out of the third theophany in Revelation 16:18, where they are separated in the judgment of the sheep (righteous) and goats (wicked) (Matt. 25:31–46). The sheep appear to be the ones who are being reigned over in the millennium.

FIGURE 31: POPULATING EARTH AND HEAVEN

End of trumpets		End of bowls	Start of millennium	End of millennium
	Seven bowls 30 days Day 1261–1290 Dan. 12:11–12	Earth restored 45 days Day 1291–1335 Dan. 12:11–12	Old earth with "twisted crust" Isa. 65:18–25 Rev. 20:1–6	New earth Isa. 65:17 Rev. 21
Day 1260	Old earth	Day 1290 Earth's crust "twisted" Isa. 24:1 Rev. 16:20	Day 1335 First population event	Great white throne Second population event

GREAT WHITE THRONE JUDGMENT AND SECOND RESURRECTION

The Great White Throne judgment in Revelation 20:11–15 is when the "rest of the dead" come back to life, as described in Revelation 20:5, which occurs at the end of the millennium. The resurrection to judgment is expected to occur as described in John 5:29: "those who have done evil to the resurrection of judgment."

The sheep who come out of the millennium and their children would also need to be judged. John 5:28b–29 says, "an hour is coming when all who are in the tombs will hear his voice and come out, those who have done good to the resurrection of life, and those who have done evil to the resurrection of judgment." Revelation 20:12b says: "Then another book was opened, which is the book of life." So it appears both the book of life and book of judgment are opened during the Great White Throne judgment.

> The rest of the dead did not come to life until the thousand years were ended. (Rev. 20:5a)

> Then I saw a great white throne and him who was seated on it. From his presence earth and sky fled away, and no place was found for them. And I saw the dead, great and small, standing before the throne, and books were opened. *Then another book was opened, which is the book of life.* And the dead were judged by what was written in the books, according to what they had done. And the sea gave up the dead who were in it, Death and Hades gave up the dead who were in them, and they were judged, each one of them, according to what they had done. Then Death and Hades were thrown into the lake of fire. This is the second death, the lake of fire. And if anyone's name was not found written in the book of life, he was thrown into the lake of fire. (Rev. 20:11–15, emphasis added)

SECOND POPULATION EVENT

The second population event occurs after the millennium and Great White Throne judgment are over. The apostle John "saw a new heaven and a new earth, for the first heaven and the first earth had passed away, and the sea was no more. And I saw the holy city, new Jerusalem, coming down out of heaven from God, prepared as a bride adorned for her husband" (Rev. 21:1–2).

MILLENNIUM: LIFE ON EARTH

Isaiah 65:21 says, "They shall build houses and inhabit them; they shall plant vineyards and eat their fruit." Zephaniah 3:9 says, "For at that time I will change the speech of the peoples to a pure speech, that all of them may call upon the name of the LORD and serve him with one accord."

The sheep from the third theophany will have long lives, though they will eventually die a physical death (Isa. 65:20). It seems their longevity could be similar to the patriarchs of Genesis before the flood. Genesis 5:27 tells us of the oldest person who ever lived: "Thus all the days of Methuselah were 969 years, and he died." Therefore, only their children may live to the time when Satan is released again. Those resurrected during the seventieth week of Daniel will likely be unable to have children. "For in the resurrection they neither marry nor are given in marriage, but are like angels in heaven" (Matt. 22:30).

> No more shall there be in it an infant who lives but a few days, or an old man who does not fill out his days, for the young man shall die a hundred years old, and the sinner a hundred years old shall be accursed. (Isa. 65:20)

MILLENNIUM: JUDICIAL SYSTEM

The glory of the Lord will fill the fourth temple, as described in Ezekiel 42:1–9. Peace on earth will exist until Satan is released at the end of his thousand years. During the millennium, the Lord "shall not judge by what his eyes see, or decide disputes by what his ears hear" (Isa. 11:3b). His wisdom is infinitely more than King Solomon's wisdom as in 1 Kings 3:16–28. Perhaps only complex issues, such as disagreements between nations, would need his resolution. Revelation 20:4–5 has the others sitting on thrones reigning with Christ. This efficient, tiered judicial system is analogous to Moses in Exodus 18 having those assisting him in less complicated cases. The initial judicial workload is expected to be small until the sheep from the third theophany begin having children.

MILLENNIUM: JERUSALEM WITH TWO INLAND PORTS

Jerusalem will become a city with two opposite ports where the water flow originates from the fourth temple. Ezekiel 47:3–5 describes a river as it grows in size from its source in Jerusalem to the east for four thousand cubits, which is about seven thousand feet. At that point Ezekiel could not pass through. It is described as being a large and deep body of water, such as a port. "Living waters shall flow out from Jerusalem, half of them to the eastern sea and half of them to the western sea. It shall continue in summer as in winter" (Zech. 14:8). So Jerusalem will have two year-round ports. Having two ports on direct opposite sides of a city so far inland is unique in the world. This source of living water from the temple seems to be a geographical representation of Ezekiel 38:12, where Jews in Israel "dwell at the center of the earth." The leaves of the trees along the banks of the living waters will be used for healing and their fruit for food (Ezek. 47:12). When countries come to Jerusalem with gifts for Jesus, it could be expected they would take a few back home for those in need of healing.

MILLENNIUM: TEMPLE SACRIFICES BEGIN AGAIN

During the millennium, the Feasts of the Lord will begin again, with daily animal sacrifices and grain offerings performed by Jewish priests at the Jerusalem temple. There will be one new feast and three existing Old Testament feasts. The new feast will be in the spring on the first day of the first month (Nisan) (Ezek. 45:18; Zech. 14:16). This first feast of the millennium will start on the first day of the millennium (Ezek. 45:18–19). Passover will continue to occur on the fourteenth day of the first month (Lev. 23: 5–6; Ezek. 45:21–24). Unleavened Bread will continue to start on the fourteenth day of the first month, lasting seven days (Lev. 23:6–8; Ezek. 45:21–24). Tabernacles (Booths) will also continue to start the fifteenth day of the seventh month (Tishri) (Num. 29:12; Ezek. 45:25; Zech. 14:16). Both the Passover and Tabernacles are a seven-day holiday. So there appears to be three spring feasts and one fall feast in the millennium. Leviticus and Numbers initially established four spring feasts and three fall feasts. There is no mention of any feast being celebrated after the millennium in Revelation 21.

HOW LONG IS SATAN ON THE EARTH DURING THE MILLENNIUM?

Revelation 20:3 tells us Satan's duration on the earth during the millennium will be a "little while." An angel "threw him into the pit, and shut it and sealed it over him, so that he might not deceive the nations any longer, until the thousand years were ended. After that he must be released for a little while." Since the time that Satan is shut up in the pit and the time earth is populated are the same duration of a thousand years, the duration of this "little while" can be determined.

During the sixth poured bowl, there is the battle of Armageddon (Rev. 16:12–16; 19:11–21). During this battle, the beast (the man of lawlessness) is captured and thrown into the lake of fire (Rev. 19:20). This author believes at that same moment Satan may be bound in the bottomless pit on a great chain for a thousand years (Rev. 20:1–2). If not, then Satan, a spirit being, could again roam the earth causing warfare. Nowhere in Scripture is there any warfare after the Armageddon campaign until near the end of the millennium. We saw in chapter 8 that the rapture of the seventh poured bowl might be equated to a one-day event occurring on Day 1,290. Using these calculations, the last day of the sixth poured bowl would be Day 1,289. Day 1,335 begins the millennium, when the earth's twisted crust is expected to be populated again. The difference in days between when Satan will probably be bound when the sixth bowl is poured and when the earth will be populated again seems to be about forty-six days (1,335 − 1,289). Therefore, this analysis indicates that Satan may be released back on earth for a "little while," determined to be about forty-six days before the end of the populated millennium. The next paragraph will show this definition is a larger range of days which includes forty days.

Alternatively there is nothing in Scripture that prevents the dragon (Satan) from roaming the earth from Day 1,259 to 1,260. This alternative position can be supported since the beast is captured in Revelation 19:20, though the dragon is not captured until later in Revelation 20:1–3. Therefore, the 46 days might be 45 days.

A LITTLE WHILE

"A little while" is referenced 29 times in the Bible. At least five times are in reference to a short amount of time measured in hours (1 Kings 18:45; Matt.

26:73; Mark 14:70; Acts 5:34; Heb. 10:37). Two are in reference to the fury near the end of the great tribulation (Isa. 10:25; 26:20). One was with Satan (Rev. 20:3). About eight were too difficult to determine where in prophecy they are located or even to approximate their duration.

The Scriptures remaining (John 12:35; 13:33; 14:19; 16:16–18; Heb. 2:7, 2:9) appear to have a common theme relative to the apostles not seeing Jesus again for a little while. This little while duration could have relevance to determine the duration of the fury just before the great tribulation ends. This analysis assumes the fury during the great tribulation is measured in days and not in hours. Satan's *little while* was previously in days.

It is interesting to note that Jesus used the words "a little while" in John 14:19 and 16:16–19 in reference to the time from His crucifixion until His ascension (Acts 1:3). This duration is from the Passover meal until Jesus's ascension, which would be forty days. *The John MacArthur ESV Study Bible* has the following commentary on John 16:16–18's "a little while":

> The first reference is plainly to the brief period between the crucifixion and the resurrection of Jesus, and the second reference is to the resurrection appearances (the "little while" after which the disciples will see Jesus again). The phrase is repeated by both Jesus and the disciples (vv. 17–19), recalling four previous instances of "a little while" in John's Gospel (cf. 7:33; 12:35; 13:33; 14:19).[2]

We now recognize that these forty days and the previous paragraph of Satan being loosed for forty–five or forty–six days provides some confidence of what the definition of "a little while" generally means.

> Yet a *little while* and the world will see me no more, but you will see me. Because I live, you also will live. (John 14:19, emphasis added)

> A *little while*, and you will see me no longer; and again a little while, and you will see me. (John 16:16, emphasis added)

---

2   John MacArthur ESV Study Bible, Crossway, Wheaton, Illinois, © 2008, 2234.

[An angel] threw [Satan] into the pit, and shut it and sealed it over him, so that he might not deceive the nations any longer, until the thousand years were ended. After that he must be released for a *little while*. (Rev. 20:3, emphasis added)

PERSECUTION GETS WORSE JUST BEFORE IT ENDS

Isaiah 26:19–21 references a coming resurrection and, though before it comes, the persecution gets much worse, which is called the fury. Earlier it was shown the fourth opened seal was the tribulation, which leads to the fifth opened seal of the great tribulation, and then into the sixth opened seal when the tribulation ends.

In v. 20, the fury is so bad that the Lord requests that his people hide in their chambers, likely with their doors locked, for *a little while* until it has passed. When it ends the great tribulation seems to be over. It is not reasonable to interpret this fury as ending after the fourth opened seal of tribulation since the fifth opened seal of the great tribulation follows it.

Previously this *little while* duration was forty to forty–six days, then the persecution would end. In chapter 3, it was shown that the great tribulation will end with the opening of the sixth seal. Therefore, it seems that just before the great tribulation ends the persecution will worsen for about forty to forty–six days. Statistically, using a few data points would provide an extremely low level of confidence, though considering the alternative this general guidance about how to mitigate martyrdom is significantly better than not having any understanding of what might unfold.

Of course, it would be extremely valuable to know when the fury might begin to start hiding. My next book will hopefully answer this question.

Jesus' response phrase to those martyred is to wait under the altar "a little longer" until others are martyred (Revelation 6:11). This is a reference to the last verse of the fifth opened seal of the great tribulation. These additional martyred to join them could be representative of the fury increasing before the great tribulation ends. Though "a little longer" does not exactly match the fury reference of "a little while", the chronological context appears to be relevant.

Then they were each given a white robe and told to rest a *little longer*, until the number of their fellow servants and their brothers should be complete, who were to be killed as they themselves had been. (Rev. 6:11, emphasis added)

Your dead shall live; their bodies shall rise. You who *dwell in the dust* (resurrection), awake and sing for joy! For your dew is a dew of light, and the earth will give birth to the dead. Come, *my* (the Lord's) people, enter your chambers, and shut your doors behind you; hide yourselves for a *little while* until the *fury* [near the end of the great tribulation] has passed by. For behold, the Lord is coming out from his place to punish the inhabitants of the earth for their iniquity, and the earth will disclose the blood shed on it, and will no more cover its slain. (Isa. 26:19–21, emphasis added).

Chapter 12

Final Thoughts

THE WAY TO SALVATION

The Word of God gives us clear directions on how to be saved—now, in the days ahead, and for eternity. Read these steps thoughtfully:

1) *All have sinned.* Romans 3:23 declares that "all have sinned and fall short of the glory of God." So to begin, admit you are a sinner.

2) *The wages of sin is death.* Romans 6:23 says, "the wages of sin is death, but the free gift of God is eternal life in Christ Jesus our Lord." Understand that as a sinner, you deserve eternal death. However, God is offering you the gift of eternal life. Tell Him you want this free gift.

3) *Confess Jesus is Lord.* Romans 10:9 says that "if you confess with your mouth that Jesus is Lord and believe in your heart that God raised him from the dead, you will be saved." Tell God and others you believe that Jesus is Lord and that God raised Him from the dead.

4) *Be Baptized.* The apostle Peter said, "Repent and be baptized every one of you in the name of Jesus Christ for the forgiveness of your sins, and you will receive the gift of the Holy Spirit" (Acts 2:38). Find a solid Bible-teaching church and get baptized to show your public profession of faith.

I would recommend you get a good study Bible. My favorite translation is the English Standard Version (ESV). The New Testament is a good location to start. Then find a good Bible study group where your faith can grow. Reading the Bible daily is important to grow your faith. "So faith comes from hearing, and hearing through the word of Christ" (Rom. 10:17). Regardless of when we think our Lord will return, we should always be ready! If you have been waiting for a wake-up call, this is it! Begin by having a relationship with Jesus, the Son of God. As your faith grows, you will begin to produce healthy fruit that shows He is working in your life.

BEARING FRUIT AND SPIRITUAL GIFTS

If we are growing in the Word, then we will bear good fruit of the Spirit and not the works of the flesh. God also desires the fruits of good works and service to others (Matt. 5:14–16; Rom. 12:6–8; Gal. 5:19–23). Determine your spiritual gifts by examining your life compared to Scripture. You can also ask a mature godly leader to help you discover your spiritual gifts. Practicing those gifts will help you bear more fruit (Rom. 12:6–8; 1 Cor. 12:8–10, 28–39).

> Now the works of the flesh are evident: sexual immorality, impurity, sensuality, idolatry, sorcery, enmity, strife, jealousy, fits of anger, rivalries, dissensions, divisions, envy, drunkenness, orgies, and things like these. I warn you, as I warned you before, that those who do such things will not inherit the kingdom of God. But the fruit of the Spirit is love, joy, peace, patience, kindness, goodness, faithfulness, gentleness, self-control; against such things there is no law. (Gal. 5:19–23)

REVIEWING THE STRENGTH OF THE NEW PREWRATH POSITION

The scriptural strength of this new prewrath position cannot be understated. In back-to-back passages, we find a rapture theophany (Rev. 8:5) and the wrath of God (Rev. 8:6–7ff.). In Luke 17:26–27b, during the Olivet Discourse, Jesus referenced the days of Noah in Genesis 7:12–13. This reference points to the first eschatological rapture and the wrath of God occurring on the same day. The back-to-back Scriptures in Revelation 8 *strongly* support this.

There are three unique phrases of "peals of thunder, rumblings, flashes of lightning, and an earthquake," which are associated with the Lord's prescience (Rev. 4:5–11, without an earthquake) and therefore a rapture. Lightning was proposed as the means of being taken (raptured) to meet Jesus in the sky. There already exists two strong prewrath proofs which must occur before Day 1 in 2 Thessalonians 2:2–5. This and other chapter 3 reasons provide an extremely strong rapture view.

None of the other four rapture positions described in chapter 1 have as much scriptural support as this new Beyond Prewrath position. Unfortunately, this portends that Christians, whether they are ready or not, will become revivalist preppers (unless they apostatize and then spend eternity in hell).

THE DISLIKED BEYOND PREWRATH POSITION

All new theological understandings are initially considered heretical. I expect this to be no different with the Beyond Prewrath position, especially since it includes proposed durations of the sixth and seventh opened seals. I do expect that over time, there will be a slow movement to it from other premillennial and amillennial positions.

About ten years ago, the Baptist Theological Seminary, and perhaps some other seminaries, would only hire professors if they had a pretribulation position, though this may have changed since then. A huge step to presenting three of the most accepted premillennial positions was made in 2010 with the book publication of *The Rapture: Pretribulation, Prewrath, or Posttribulation* by Dr. Craig Blaising, Dr. Alan Hultberg, and Dr. Douglas J. Moe.

Why would a seminary only hire professors with a pretribulation view? Perhaps many churches are unwilling to have a pastor with a strong conviction that the church will live through the great tribulation. Imagine a new pastor who begins to discuss with the congregation a concern for them to prepare for the worst and hope for the best. Preparing for the worst could include storing up extra food, medicine, consumable items, moving into the rural countryside, and basically being as self–sufficient as possible for a few years. Some in the church would not want to hear this and would leave to find another church home. Many churchgoers would wonder how an all–loving God could have the church enter a great tribulation. No church wants to lose members.

Any church that does not present all viable premillennial positions of a physical rapture to their members is doing the church body a disservice. The church should examine prophetic scripture and compare it frequently to current world events in and around Israel to see if the seventieth week of Daniel has begun. It would be wise to have each church or group of churches host a class about, and/or have a team of knowledgeable eschatological individuals alert to, the impending danger of the start of the seventieth week.

If they recognize the seventieth week has started, then the pretribulation position is no longer a viable premillennial position. At that moment, the church leadership would need to notify the church body so they can prepare, in earnest, to live through the tribulation followed by the great tribulation. This would be a once–in–a–lifetime church event, though bold leadership within the church is needed. This warning to the church body would minimize the loss of life, whether from martyrdom or falling away from the faith by taking the mark of the beast. There would also be an urgency to reach those who have not accepted Jesus as their Lord.

REVIVALIST PREPPERS

This position points to the elect having to live through the tribulation of the fourth opened seal and then the great tribulation of the fifth opened seal before being raptured. Being watchful and recognizing the day when the seventieth week begins will be valuable. This will provide Christians with enough time to prepare in advance. Those Christians who do not apostatize will be unable to buy or sell (Rev. 13:17). Consider how many things we take for granted buying: food, electricity, fuel, medicine, municipal water, medical care, medicine, clothing, and telephone service. Also, this could prevent those without the mark of the beast from paying property taxes. "And because lawlessness will be increased, the love of many will grow cold. But the one who endures to the end will be saved" (Matt. 24:12–13). Amazingly the Scriptures support us being preppers in Matthew 24:45. The reference to "his household" means we should be prepared to help with the needs of others besides our own household. If we are faithful in this, then we will be blessed. "But if anyone does not provide for his relatives, and especially for members of his household, he has denied the faith and is worse than an unbeliever" (1 Tim. 5:8).

> Who then is the faithful and wise servant, whom his master has set over *his household*, to give them their food at the proper time? *Blessed is that servant whom his master will find so doing when he comes.* Truly, I say to you, he will set him over all his possessions. (Matt. 24:45–47, emphasis added)

WHEN IS ACTION IS REQUIRED?

The first question many ask is when they need to take action. My response is to pray, wait, and stay alert to what is happening in Israel and those countries around it. If there is a multinational treaty signed with Israel for seven years, according to Daniel's counting, then that would likely indicate the start of the seventieth week of Daniel. Chapter 2 discussed that one year in Daniel is 360 days. When the first seal is opened, we should recognize the prophetic events occurring before us. This will give us confidence in making a life-changing decision to start preparing to live through the tribulation and the great tribulation. When we enter the seventieth week of Daniel, my opinion is that we will have about ten or eleven months to prepare during the first opened seal. This approximation is derived by simply dividing forty-two months by the four opened seals, assuming each is approximately the same length. As discussed in chapter 6, the first opened seal is described as a peaceful conquest, which is not likely to disturb the world's relatively peaceful condition. In our world of commerce using computers, ten or eleven months to get prepared should be enough time. Can someone wait until the second opened seal of wars and rumors of war? Perhaps, though if you live within the boundary of those at war then this is unlikely. The third opened seal of famines and earthquakes in various parts of the world would likely make preparations impossible.

HOW LONG IS SATAN'S GREAT TRIBULATION?

The second question many ask is how long Satan's great tribulation will last We know it is bound by the second half of the seventieth week of Daniel, 1,260 days. The 1,260 days is composed of the fifth to seventh opened seals and the seven blown trumpets. The fifth blown trumpet is 150 days long (Rev. 9:1–11). Chapter 3 discussed the rapture in the seventh open seal, occurring on either the seventh or eighth day. Chapter 4 discussed the sixth opened seal as possibly being between twenty-seven and thirty-two days. This reduces the length of the great tribulation to less than 1,100 days. We also know "if those days had not been cut short, no human being would be saved. But for the sake of the elect those days will be cut short" (Matt. 24:22). Not having any human being survive is a strong statement, which seems to indicate that the great tribulation will be cut short a significant amount of time. Beyond this simple analysis, the actual time is unknown.

CLOSING REMARKS

My greatest desire is to present biblical prophetic truth. However, until the seventieth week of Daniel is complete "to seal both vision and prophet" (Dan. 9:24), no one will know all of the prophetic truth. So it is necessary for each of us to study the Word of God faithfully, as the Bereans did. "Now these Jews were more noble than those in Thessalonica; they received the word with all eagerness, examining the Scriptures daily to see if these things were so" (Acts 17:11). In the same way, each of us should examine everything we hear or read and see if it aligns with what is written in the Word of God. God's word is infallible and inerrant. All human beings are fallible.

We are so blessed to have a loving God. My prayer is that you are saved and study the Scriptures diligently so that you will be on God's side in the prophetic days ahead.

Subject Index

666, 67, 105

777, 48

1948, 137

Abraham Accord, 139

Antiochus, 49–52, 128–131

baptism, 153

beast of the earth, 7, 79–80, 133–134

beast of the sea, 5–7, 15, 19–20, 65–66, 125–126, 131–134

béma, ix, 1–2, 7–8, 46–47, 115–121

Campus Crusade, 138–139

caves, 78–84

covenant of death, 70–72

cut short, 15, 18–19, 78, 157

elders, 15–16

exile, 3, 32, 83, 95, 99–101, 111–112, 118–119

false prophet, ix, 7–8, 76–77, 85–86, 88, 90, 105, 133–134, 136

false security, 83–84

false trinity, 136

fratricide, 103

Gog, 3, 24, 89–95, 102–103, 105, 130

Golden Gate, ix

half an hour, 5, 32–40, 82

hyperbole, 23, 103

idols, 78–83, 108, 154

Jacob's trouble, x, 26–27, 76–77, 95–101, 104, 111–112, 115–116, 118–119

Judas, 5, 19, 51, 126–127, 132, 136

King David, 135–136

little horn, 5–7, 19–20, 24, 29, 50, 61–62, 64–67, 70–72, 96–97, 104–105, 125–126, 130, 134

Mount of Olives, 11–12, 92–95, 101–102

Noah, 1, 31–32, 34–38, 46–47, 79–81, 85, 87, 115–116, 154

Olivet Discourse, 11–14, 13–15, 85–86, 115–116, 125–126, 128–131, 154 one hour, 65–66, 99, 130

plucked up, 64–66, 70–72

Pontius Pilate, 126–127, 136

premillennialism, 1–2, 9–20

preppers, 154, 156

put down, 64–65, 70–72, 130

rebellion, 14–17, 29, 74–77, 80, 85–86, 105

red heifer, 137, 140

sacrifice, 13–15, 24, 39, 49–54, 87, 137–138

Sinai, 39, 43, 45, 83

six acts of mercy, 118–121

son of destruction, 5–6, 19–20, 29, 65–66, 85–86, 104–105, 126–127, 131–134, 136

spiritual gifts, 116–117, 154

strong delusion, 43, 84–85

Temple Institute, 137–138

time dilation, 41–42

tribulation saints, 14, 16

two witnesses, 10–11, 26, 90, 102, 105, 115–116, 138

Scripture Index

Genesis
    5:27 147
    7:4 ....82, 109
    7:7–10 36
    7:13 36

Exodus
    23:32–33 71

Deuteronomy
    33:2 43

2 Samuel
    24:11–14...136

2 Kings
    2:11..44, 47

Job
    36:32 ....44, 46–47, 79

Isaiah
    2:9 84
    2:12 79
    2:18–19 79
    10:20–21 111
    11:3..147
    22:1 93
    24:1 141
    26:19–21 151–152
    28:15 24
    29:6 93
    33:17 93
    63:3 121
    65:17 142

Isaiah (*continued*)

65:18 142
65:20 147
65:21 147

Ezekiel

38:12 148
38:18 ....91, 102
38:19 93
38:20 93
38:21–22 103
43:6–7 145

Daniel

2:39 23
2:42 103
2:43 130
4:33 134
7:7 65
7:8 ....65, 72
7:11 62
7:12 62
7:19 ....127, 134
7:24 ....65, 71, 72, 130
8:8 64
8:9 65
8:13 53
8:13–14 49
8:14 51
8:21 ....19, 125
8:26 51
9:24 157
9:26 ....23, 25, 130, 136
9:27 ....14, 18–19, 24, 49, 67, 71, 87, 104
10:13 96
11:39..25, 65, 67, 78

Daniel (*continued*)

12:1 ....96, 100, 101
12:2–3 114
12:11–12...53

Joel

2:3 110
2:31–32 ....22, 111, 112

Habakkuk

3:11...46–47

Zephaniah

3:9 147

Zechariah

12:9–11...111
13:8 100
13:9 111
14:2 103
14:3 102
14:4 92
14:5 ....93, 94, 99
14:6–7 103
14:7 ....53, 93, 103
14:8 148
14:10 94
14:12 102–103
14:13 103

Malachi

4:5 26

Matthew

3:7 101
13:20–21 17
22:9 119
22:30 147
24:2 128–129

Matthew (*continued*)

24:3 11–12

24:4–5 72

24:6–7 72

24:7 73

24:10–11..77

24:12–13 156

24:15 ....19, 87

24:15–16 99

24:15–17 ....90–91, 94

24:21–22 ....15, 16, 78

24:22 ....19, 157

24:36 115

24:40 80

24:45–47 156

25:31–36 118

25:35 119

25:36 119

27:22 126

27:26 126–127

Mark

2:27 xii

9:41 119

Luke

10:18 45

17:24 46

17:24–26 47

17:26–27 32

17:26–30 85

17:27 80

17:28–29 33

17:34 39

21:28 39

24:50–51 92

John

    5:28–29 ....143, 146

    13:26–27 126

    14:19 150

    16:16 150

Acts

    1:11...92

    2:17–21 22

    2:38 153

    16:26 83

    17:11...157–158

    17:22–23 128

Romans

    3:23 153

    6:23 153

    9:27 ....101, 111

    10:9 153

    10:17 153

    11:11...43

    11:25–26...112

    14:10–12 116

1 Corinthians

    1:7–8 108

    3:10–15 117

2 Corinthians

    1:14 108

    5:10 116–117

Galatians

    5:19–23 154

Ephesians

    2:1–2 131

    3:6 19

Philippians

    1:6, 10 108
    2:16 108

1 Thessalonians

    4:15, 17 143–144
    4:17 ....11, 107, 145
    5:1–5 27
    5:2 109
    5:2–3 85
    5:3 ....27, 108
    5:9 ....17, 90

2 Thessalonians

    2:1–4 29
    2:3 ....75, 77, 105
    2:3–4 ....19, 85
    2:6 ....76, 104
    2:7 77
    2:7–8 91
    2:9–11...85
    2:11–12...43

1 Timothy

    4:1 ....76, 77
    4:1–2 83–84
    4:1–3 80
    5:8 156

2 Timothy

    4:3–5 86

Titus

    2:13 ....107, 120

1 John

    2:22 19

Revelation

1:7 ....43, 115
3:10 14
4:5 ....42, 115
6:1–2 72
6:3–4 73
6:5 73
6:8 131
6:11...151
6:12 39
7:9 34
7:10 ....15, 33
7:11...15
8:1 ....33, 35, 36
8:2 37
8:5 ....2, 33, 42, 43, 47, 79, 114
8:6–7 46
8:7 33
8:10 110
8:12 53–54
9:18 110
11:2...53
11:3...102
11:5...102
11:6...102
11:7...102, 133
11:13...26
11:15..134
11:17..117
11:18..116
11:19................................2, 43, 107, 114–115
12:12 96
13:1 ....19, 133
13:2 127
13:3 128
13:7 15
13:14 80

168   *Beyond Prewrath: End-Time Prophecy*

Revelation (*continued*)

13:18 ....67–68, 132
14:6–7 139
14:9 25
14:12 99
15:1 90
16:1 90
16:14 118
16:18 ....2, 43, 74, 107
16:20 144
17:8 126
17:11............................5, 19, 132
17:12 ....65, 99, 130
17:13 ....62, 136
17:13–14 130
17:16 64
17:16–17 100
19:8 118
19:14 118
19:20 ....62, 133, 134
20:3 ....149, 150–151
20:4 144
20:5 146
20:11–15..................................146
20:12 146
21:1 141
21:1–2 146–147

About the Author

Robert Parker has a Bachelor of Science in Engineering and has retired from a career as a military simulation training engineer. He is active in a local church and has a heart for construction mission trips.

You can follow Robert at www.RobertsTrumpet.com.

CPSIA information can be obtained
at www.ICGtesting.com
Printed in the USA
BVHW051318190522
637331BV00047B/213